The Greatest Name of all. The True God who alone deserves to be worshipped. This Name includes the meaning of all of His other perfect Names and Attributes

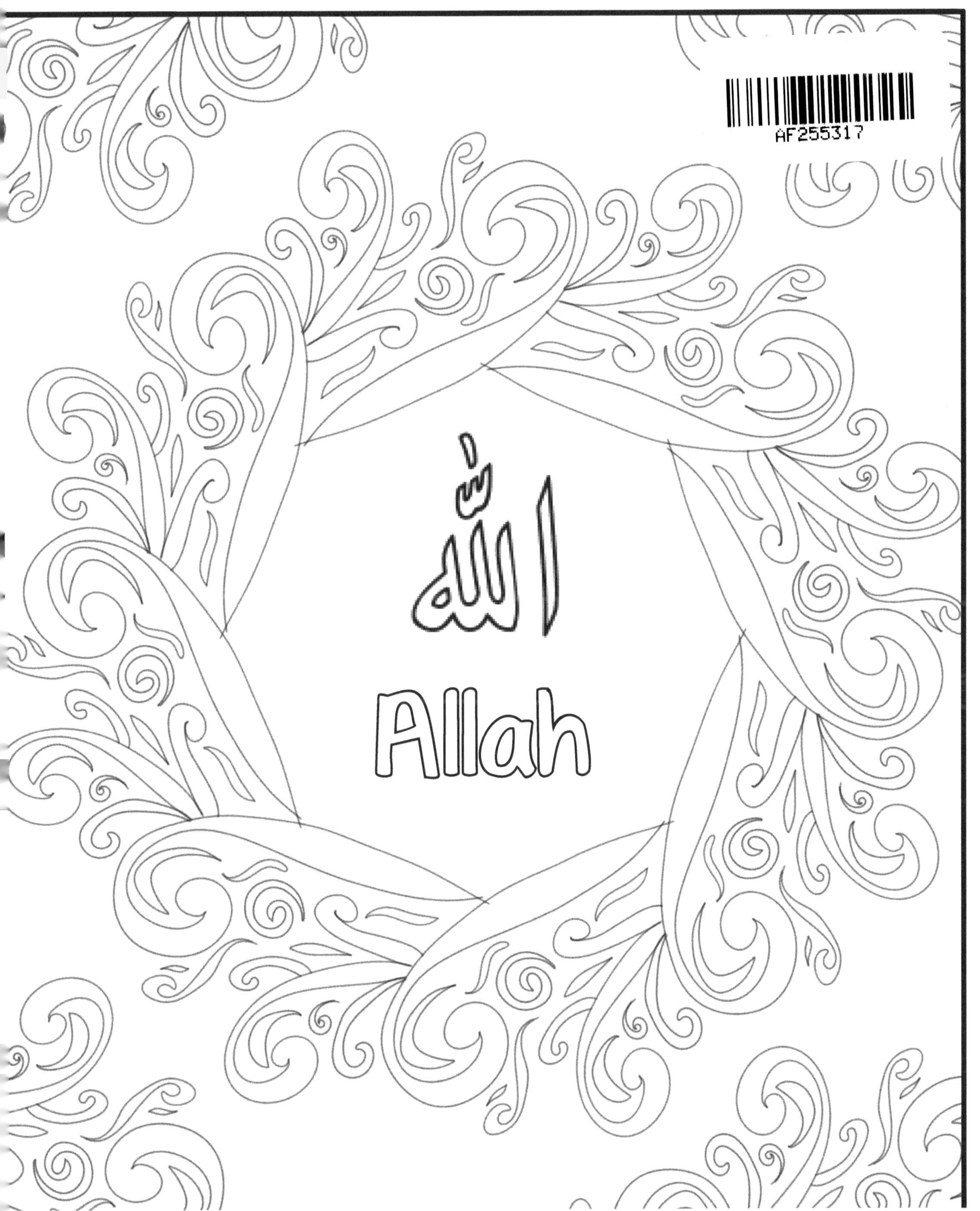

The Beneficent

He who wills goodness and mercy for all His creatures

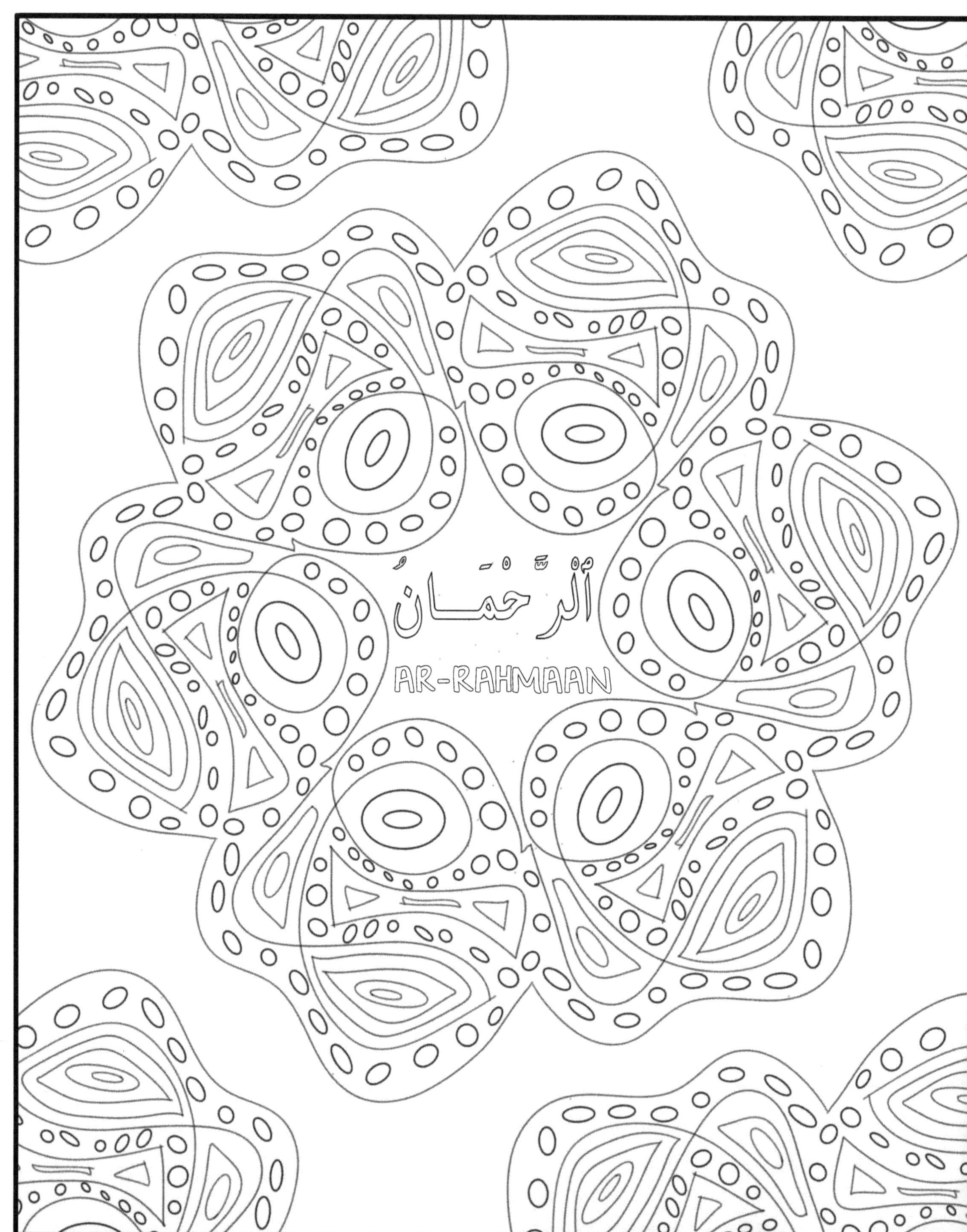

The Merciful

He who acts with extreme kindness

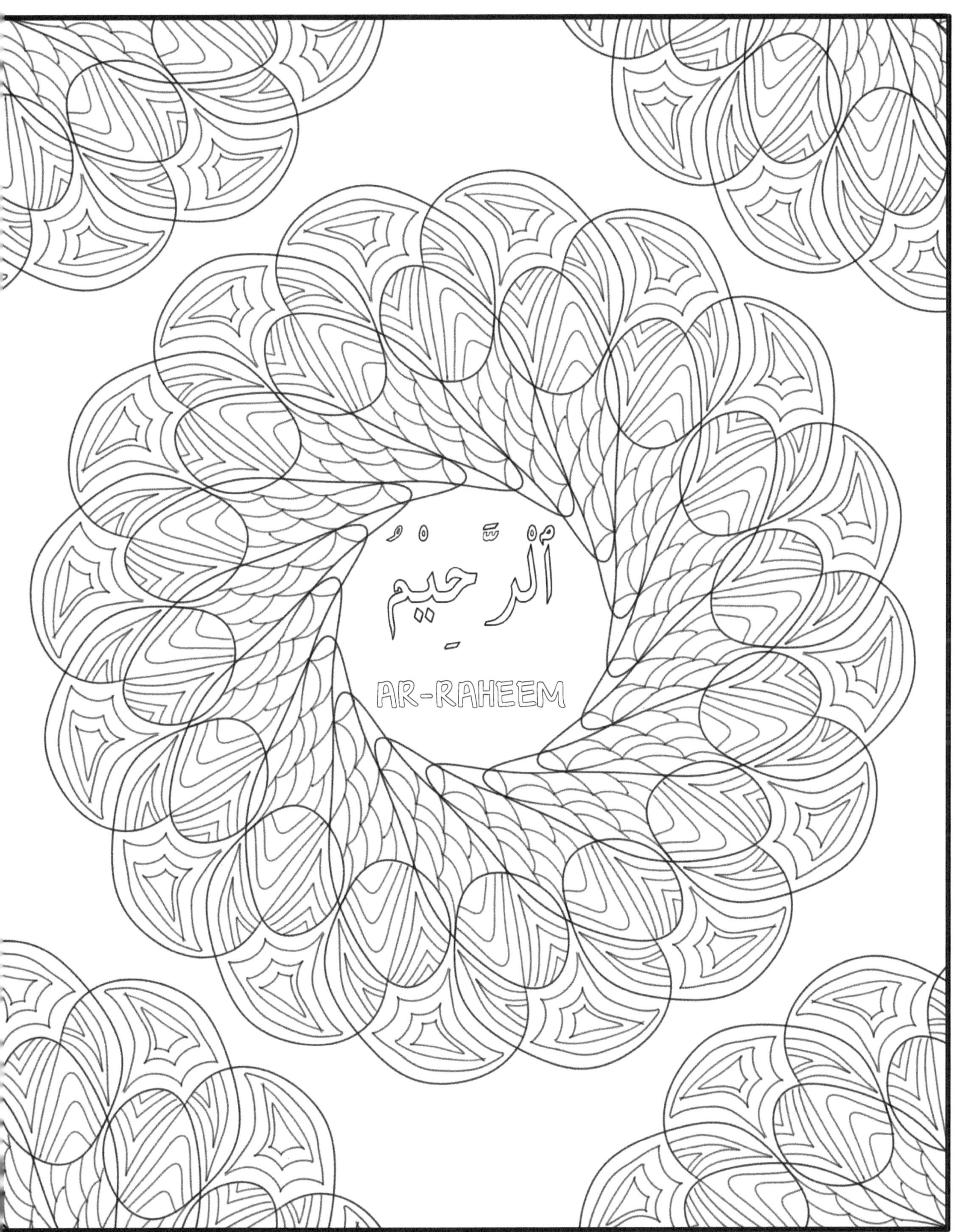

The King

The Sovereign Lord, whose Dominion is clear from imperfection

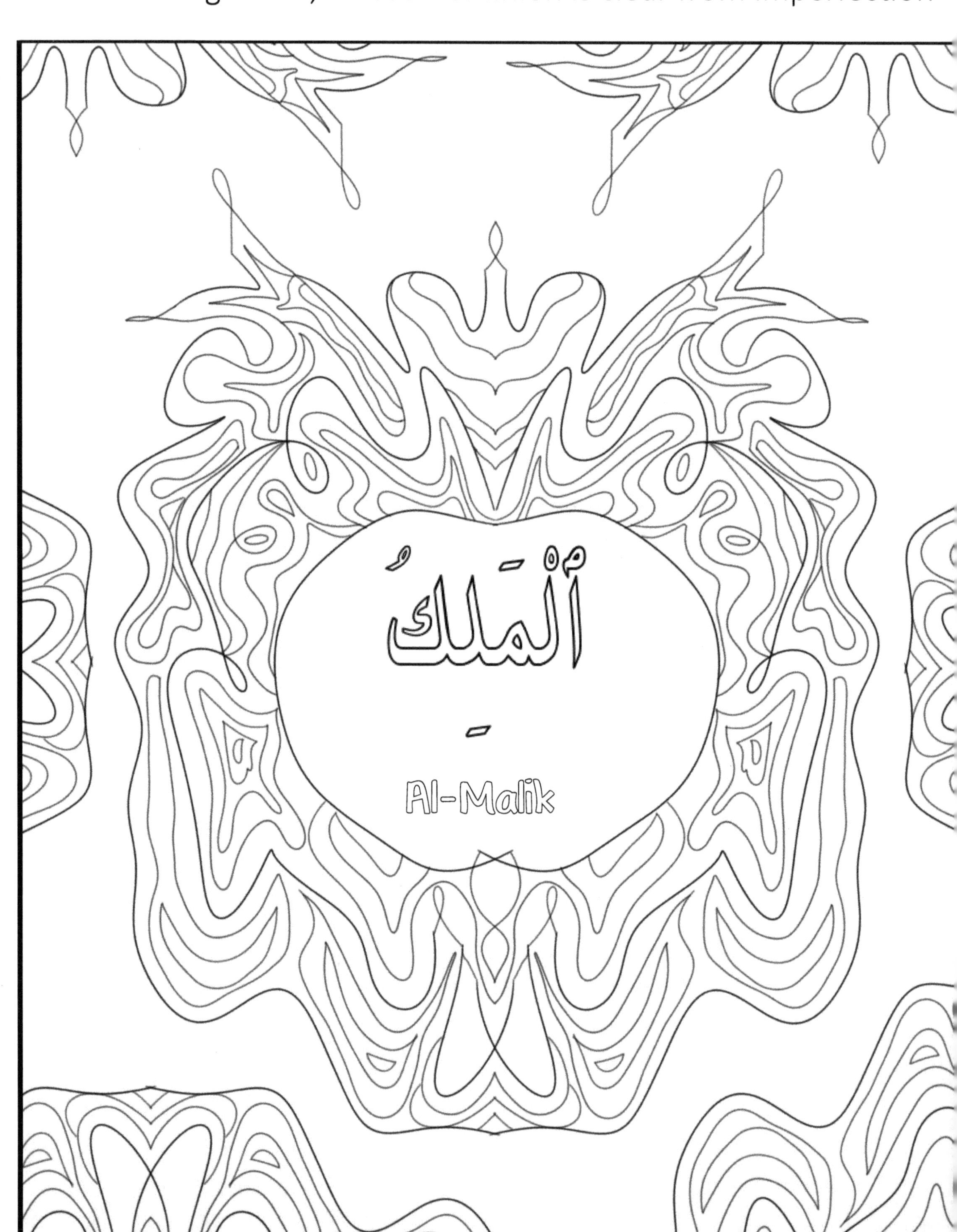

The Most Sacred

The one who is pure. He has no shortcomings, evil is not attributed to Him.

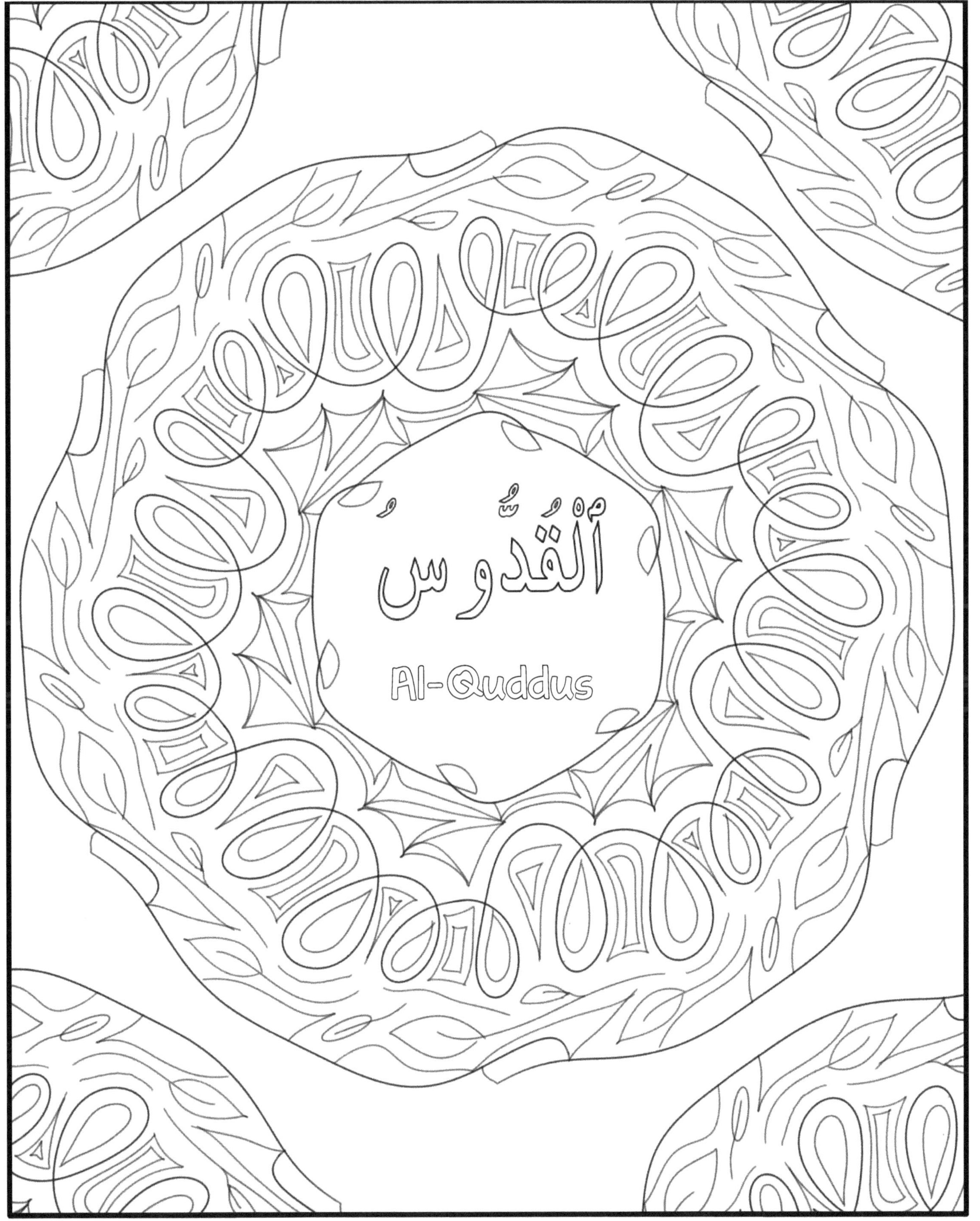

The Giver of Peace

He is free of any defect so the one who is with Him experiences tranquillity.

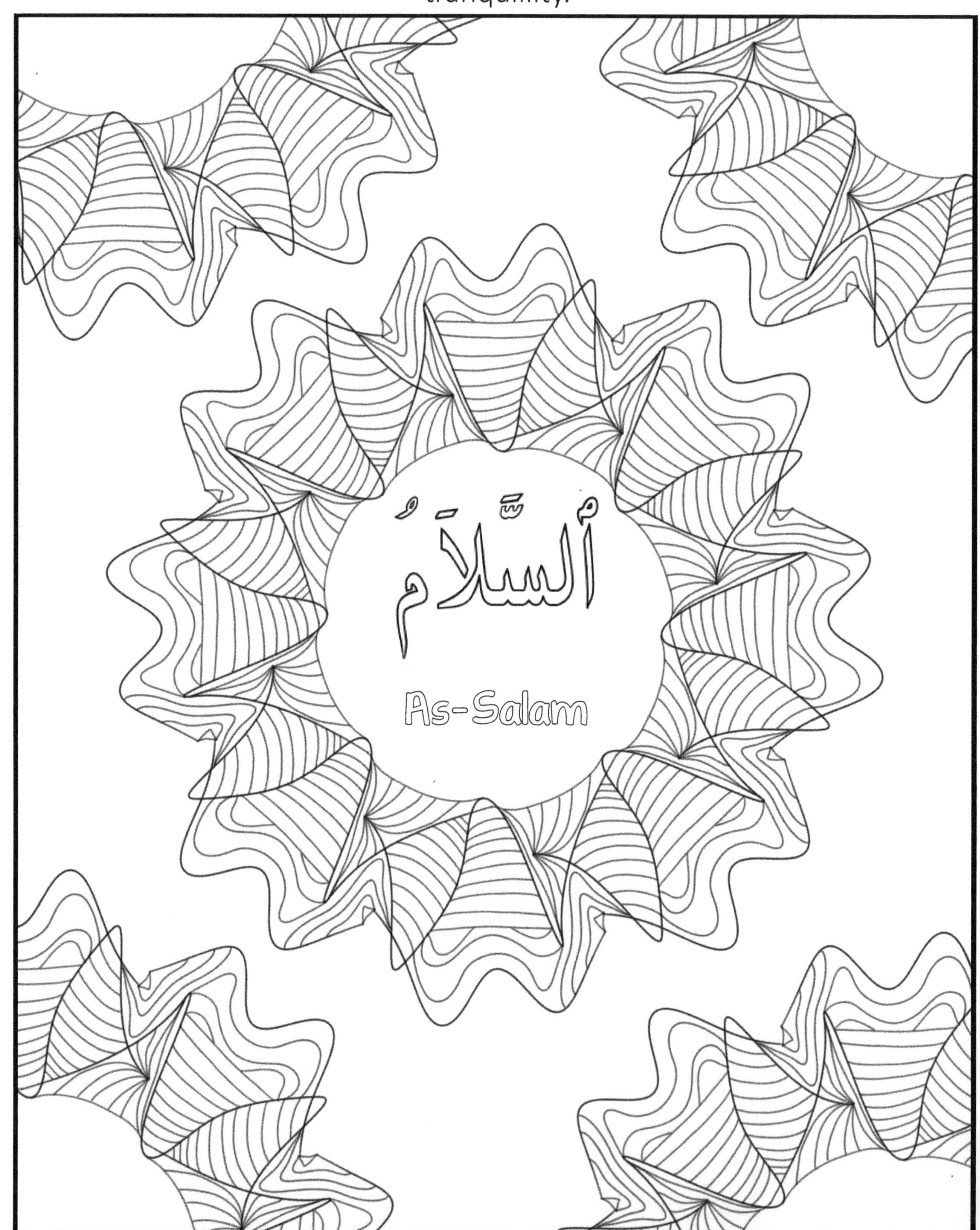

The Infuser of Faith

The One who provides peace, safety and tranquillity in the hearts of His believing servants.

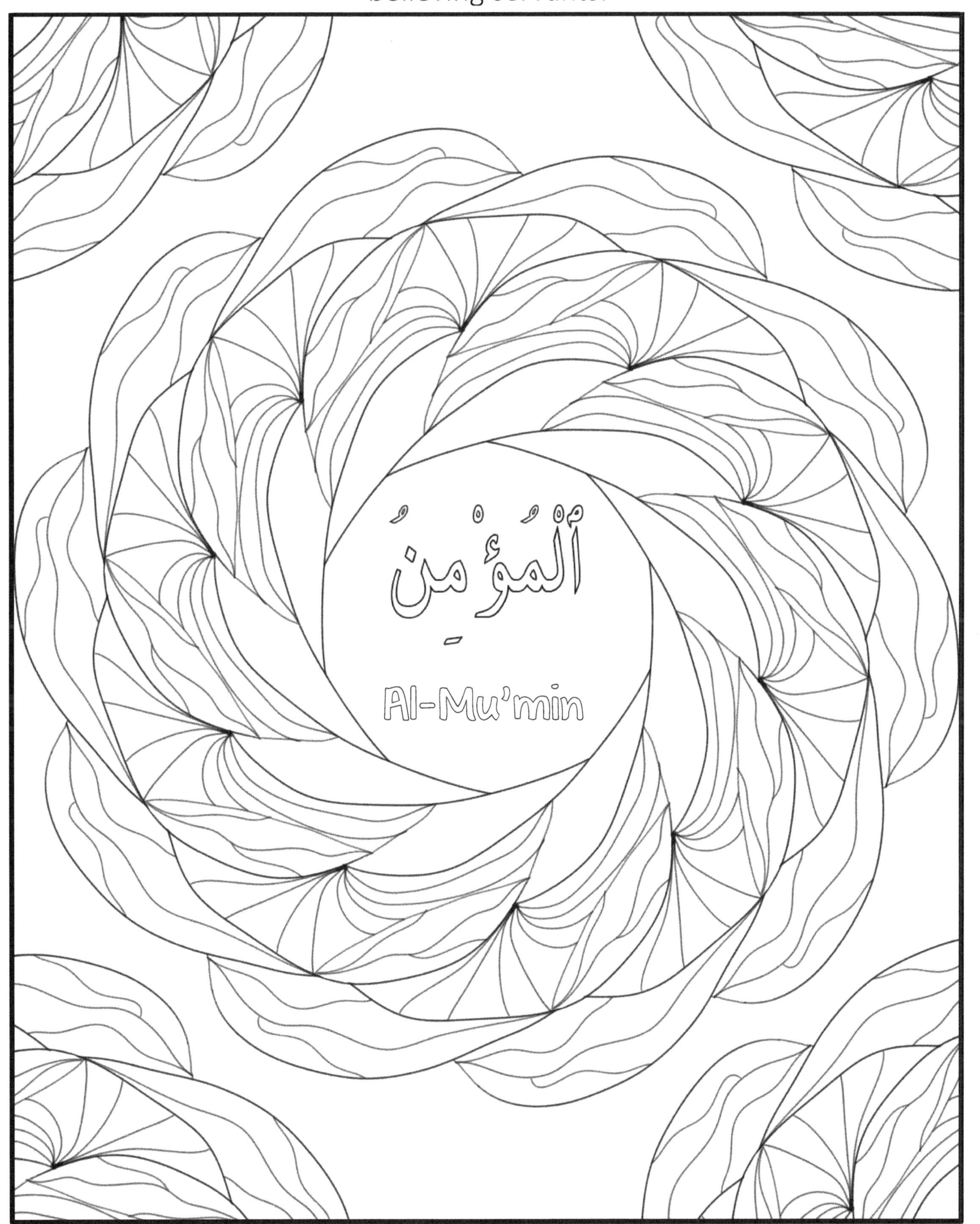

The Guardian

The One who witnesses the saying and deeds of His creatures.

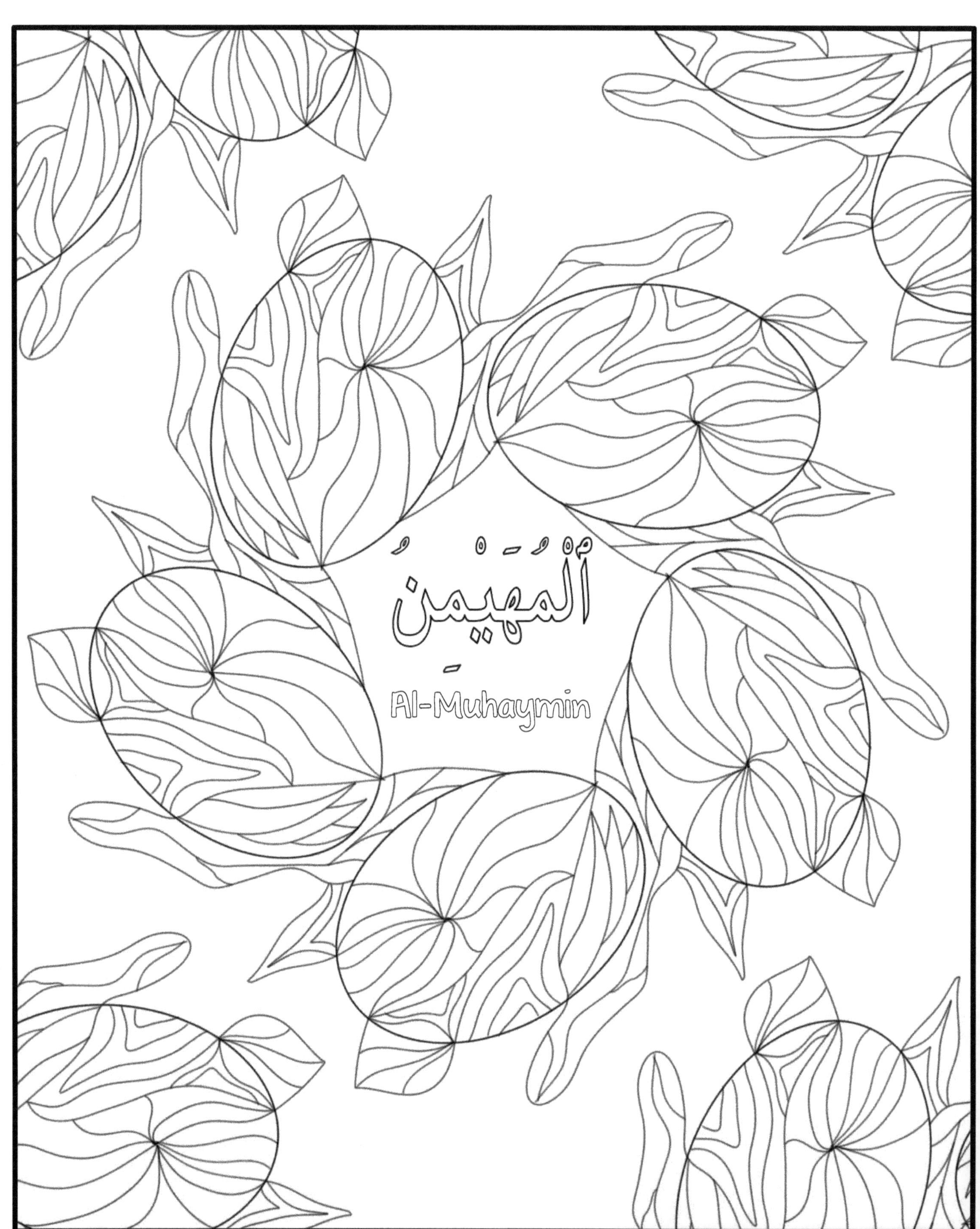

The Mighty One

The Strong, The Defeater who is not defeated.

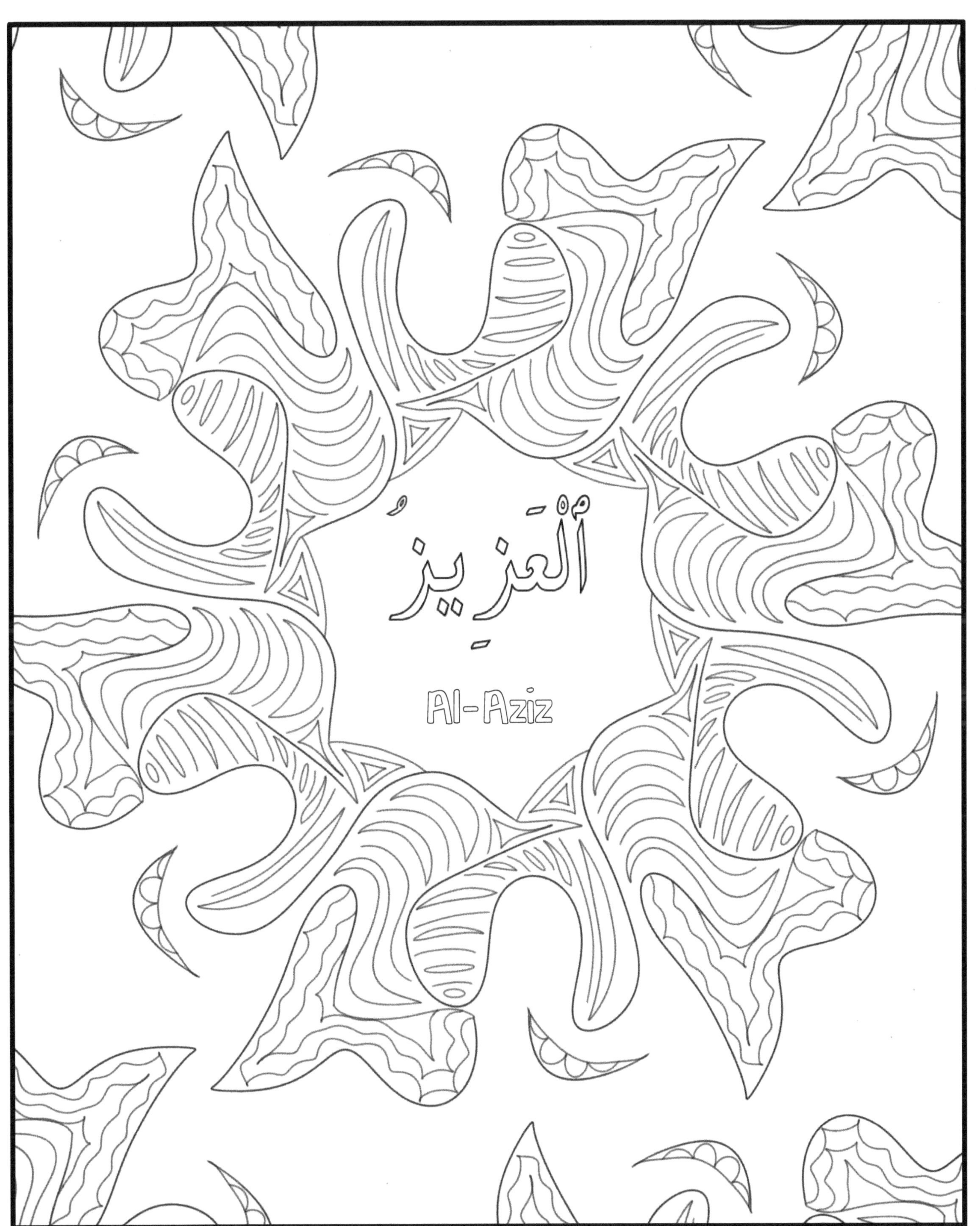

The All Compelling

The One that nothing happens in His Dominion except that which He willed

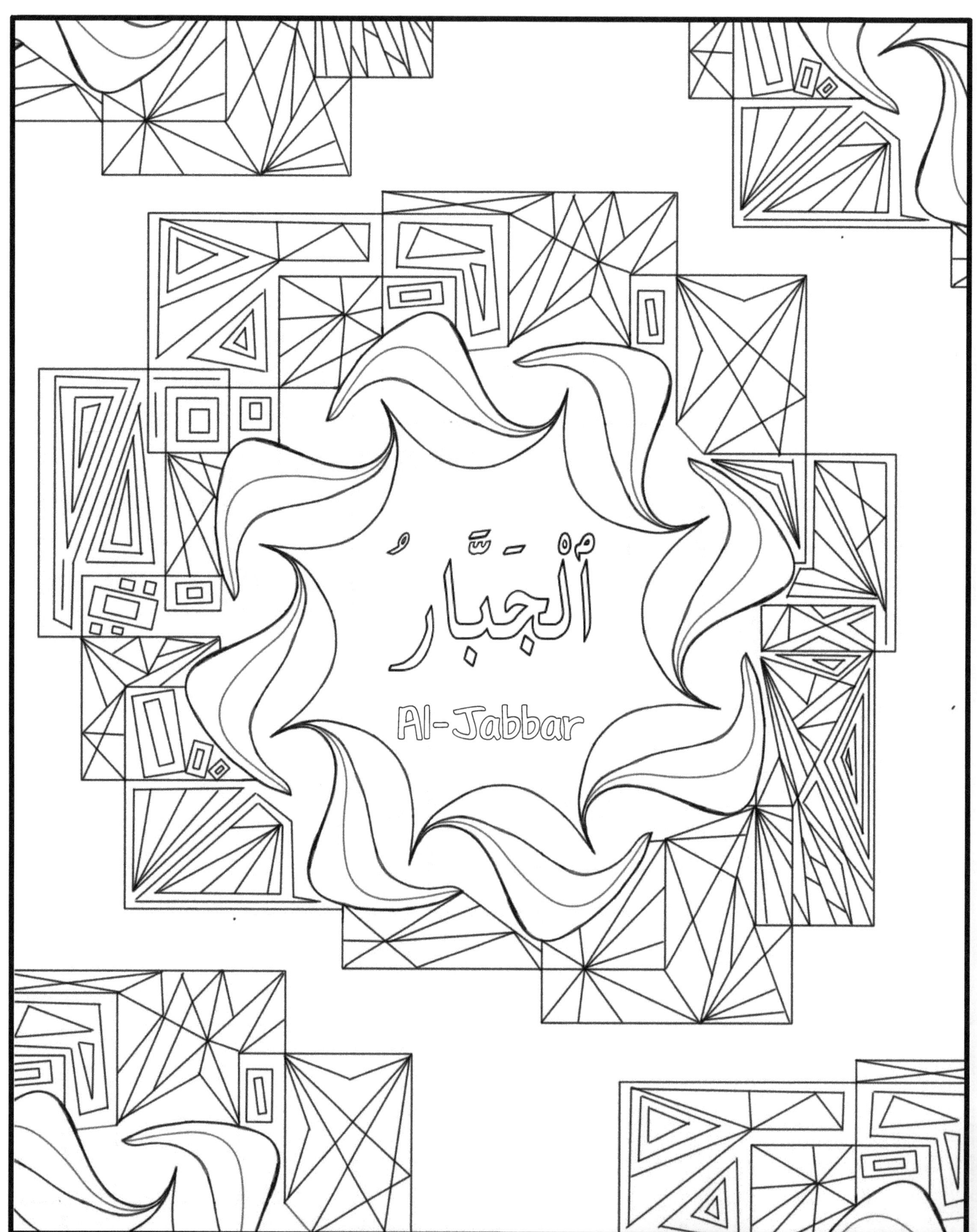

The Dominant One

The One who is clear from the attributes of the creatures and from resembling them

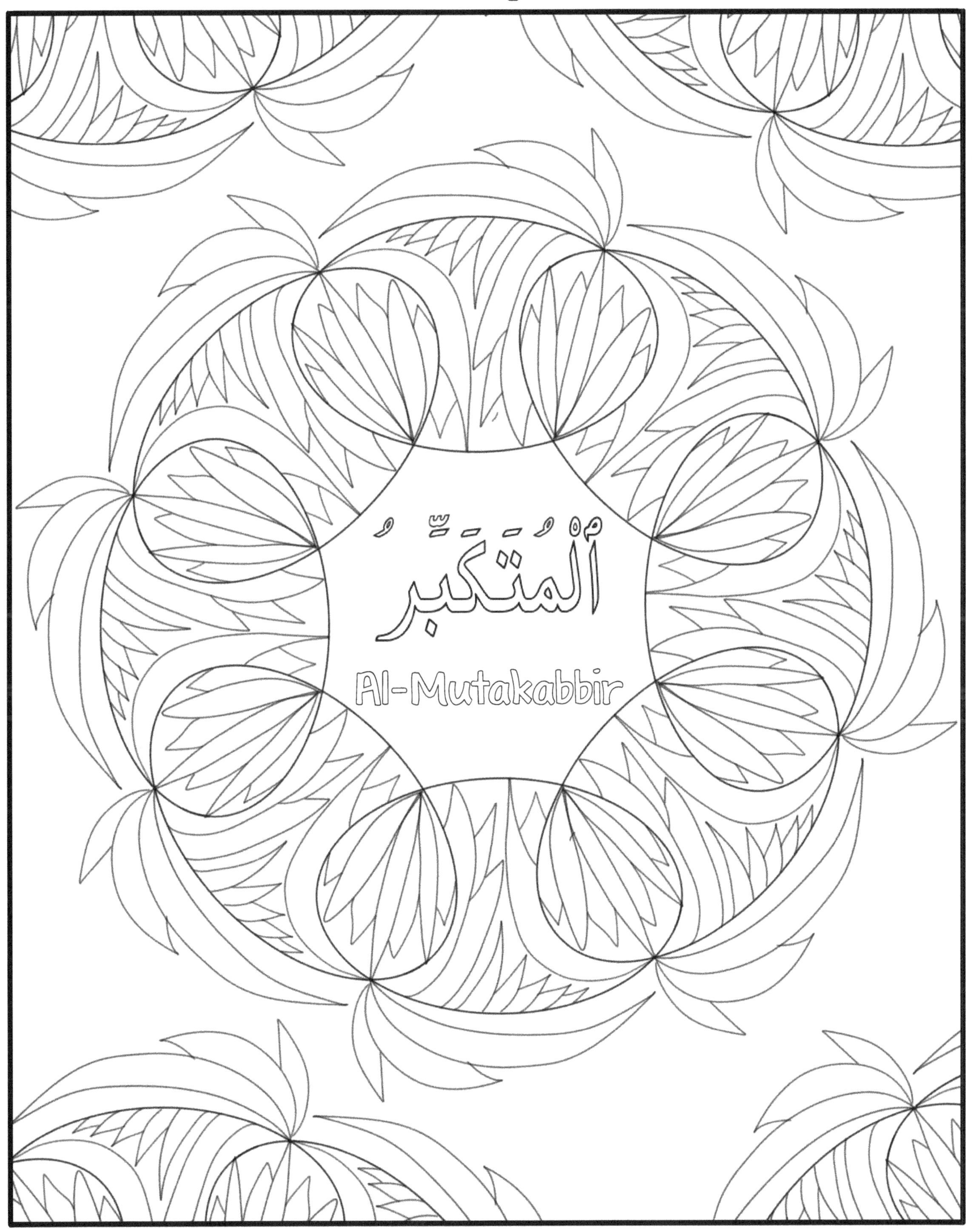

The Creator

The One who brings everything from non-existence to existence

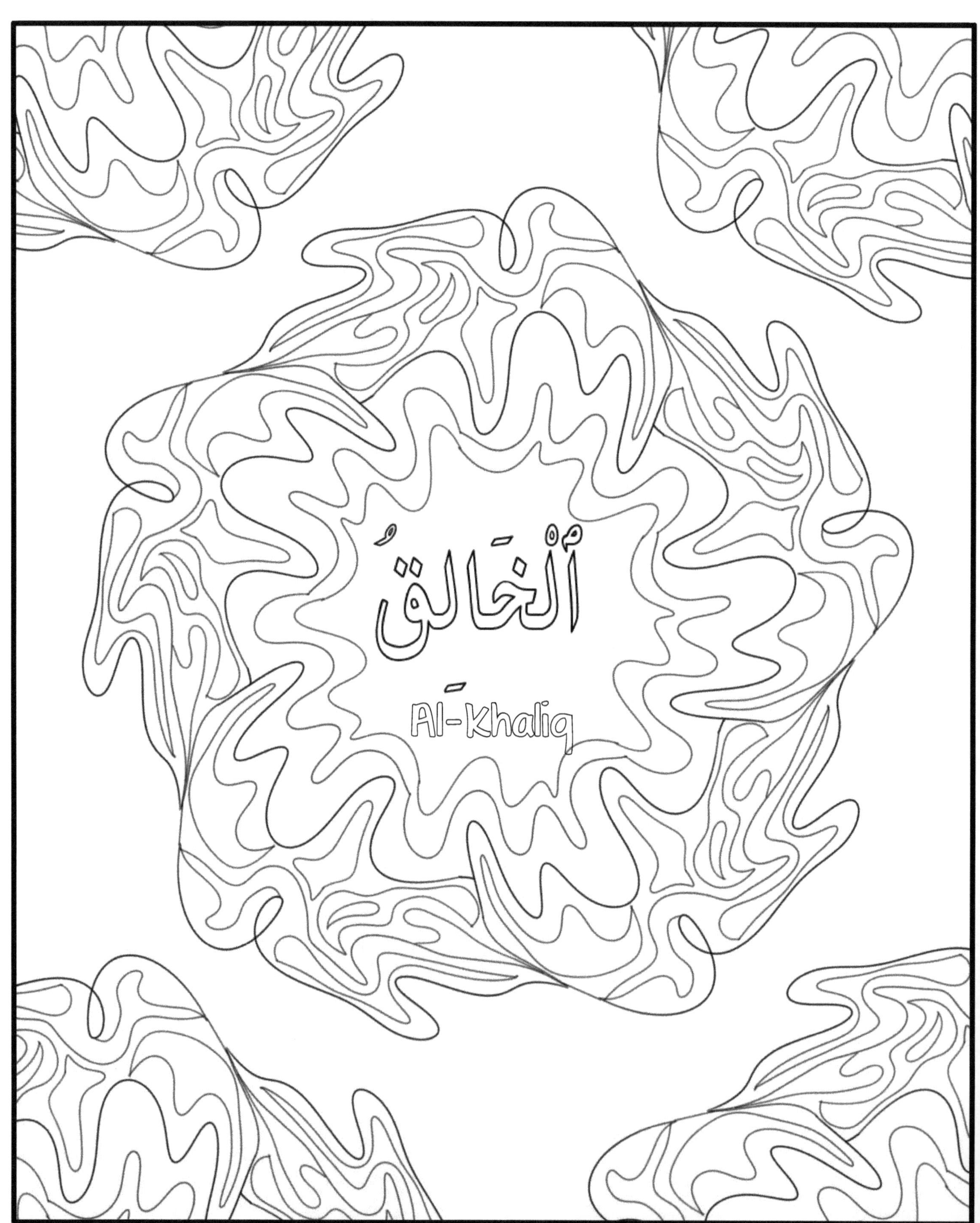

The Maker

The Maker, The Creator who has the Power to turn the entities.

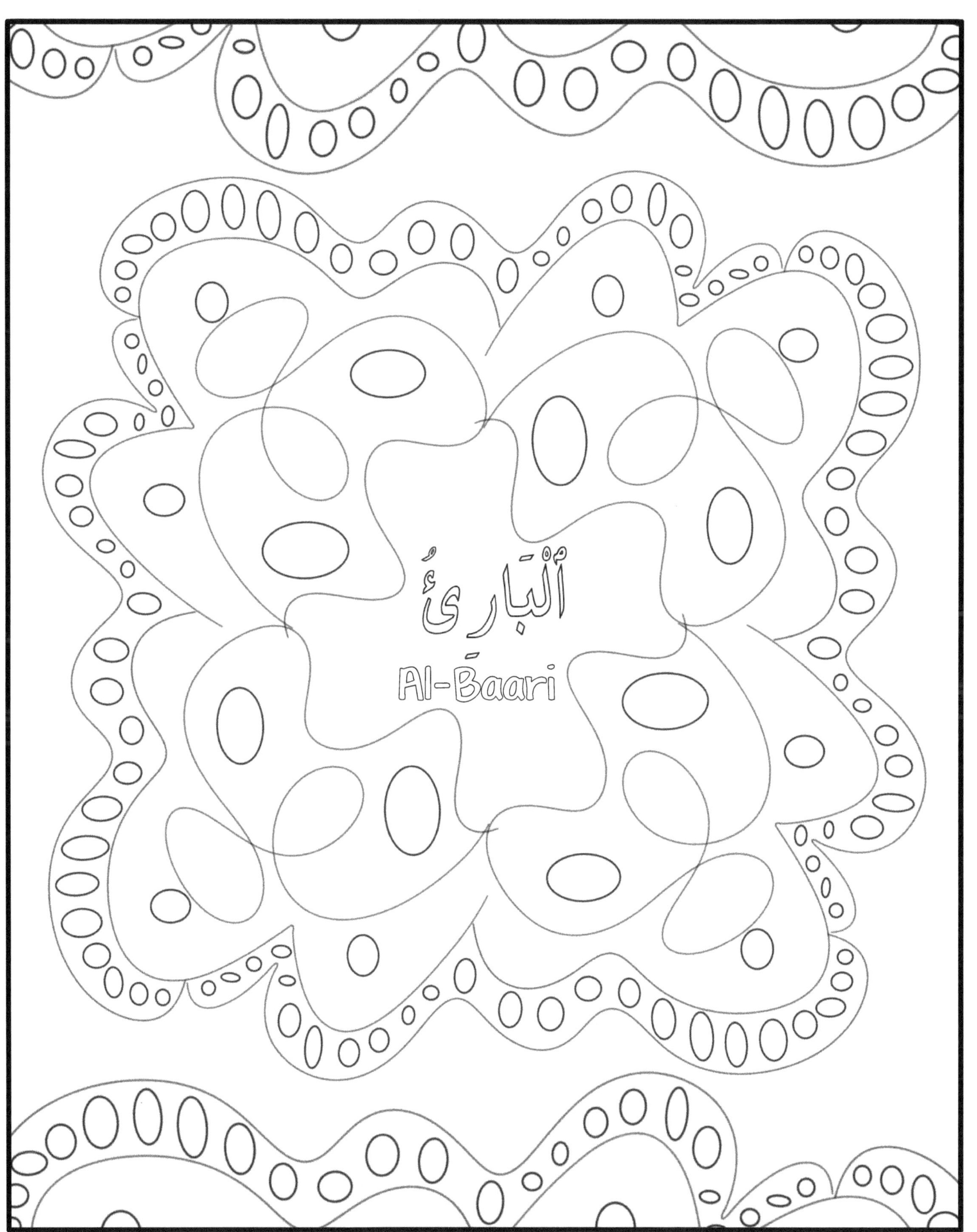

The Shaper

The One who forms His creatures in different pictures.

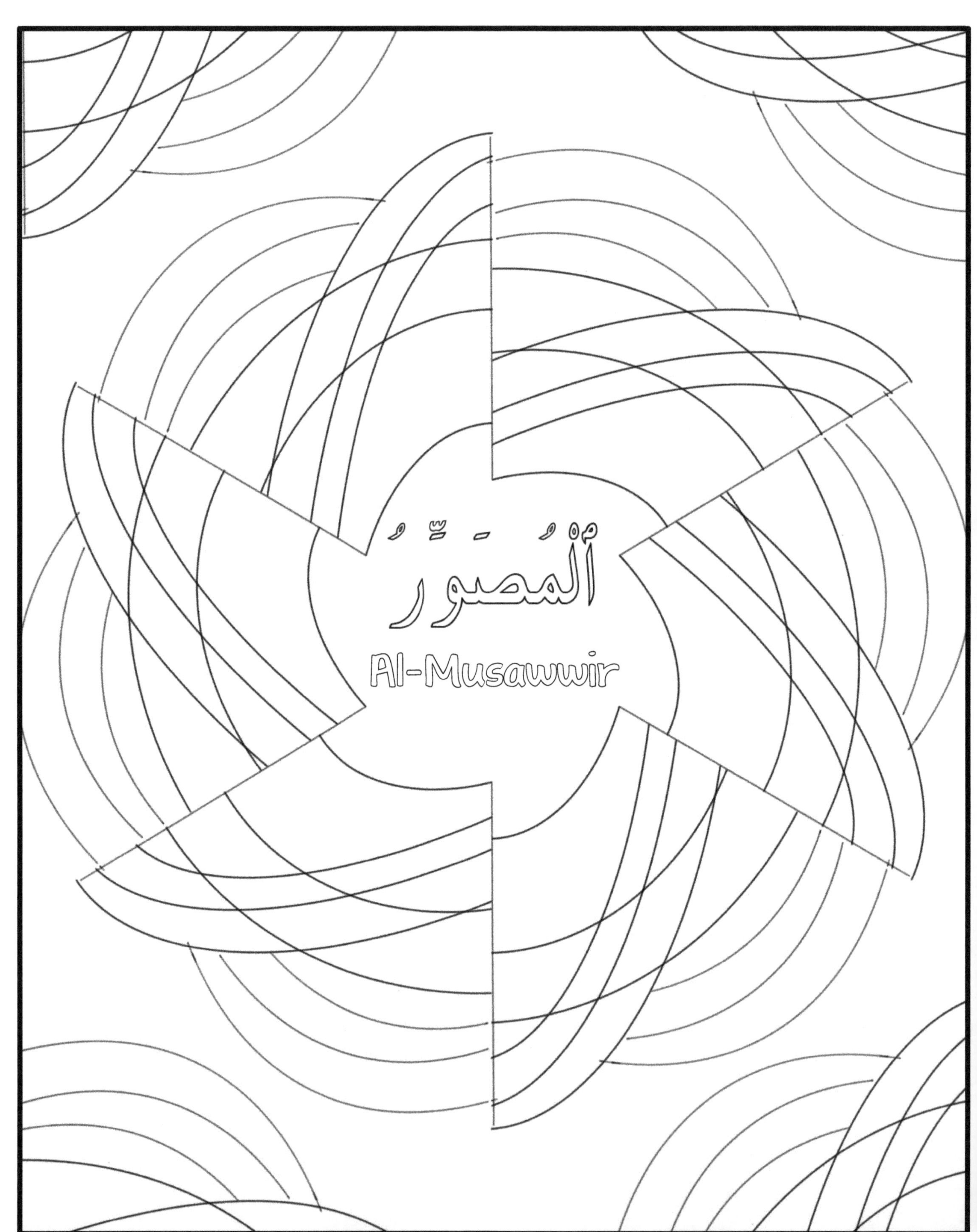

The Forgiver

The Forgiver, The One who forgives the sins of His slaves time and time again.

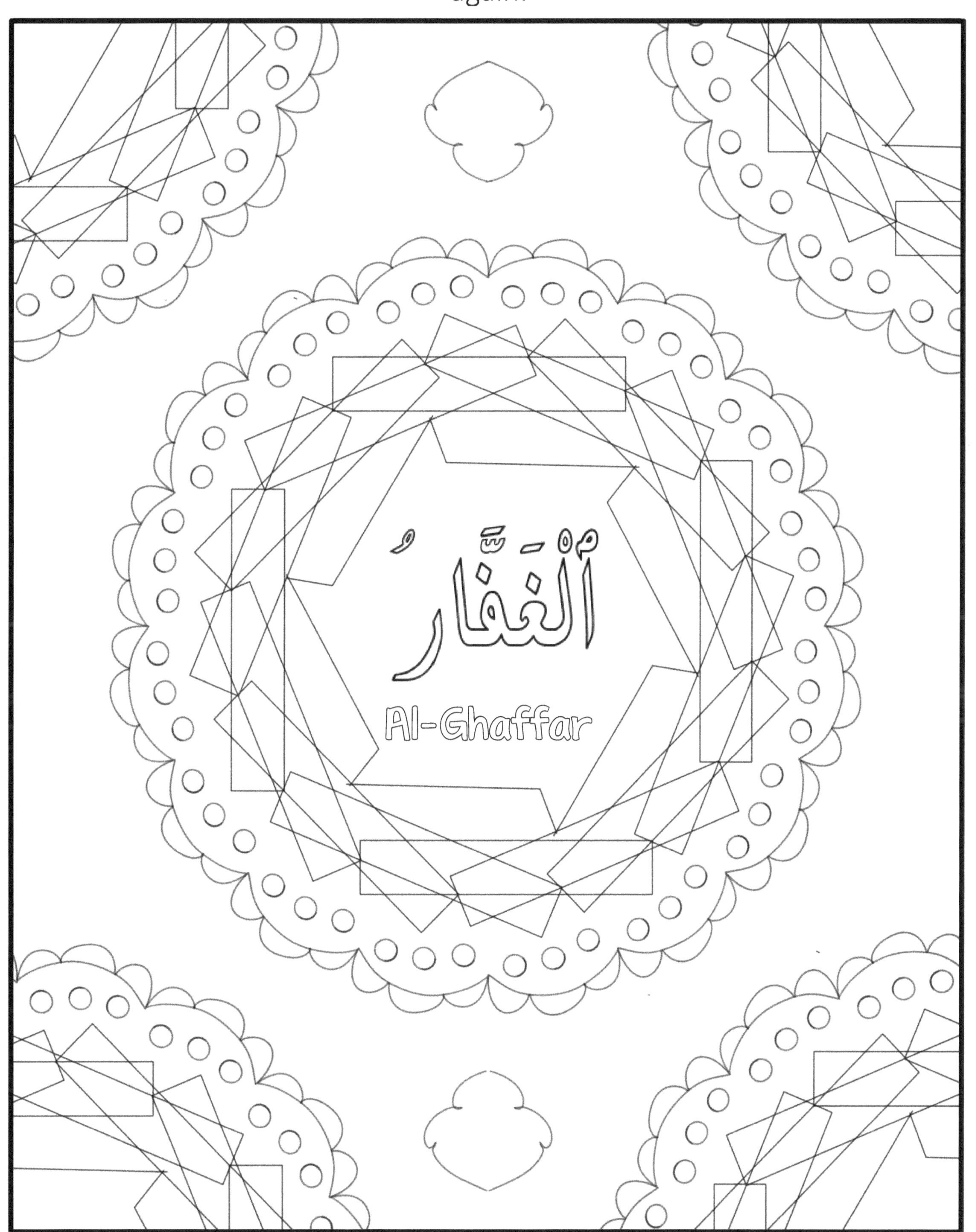

The All Prevailing

The Dominant, The One who has the perfect Power and is not unable over anything.

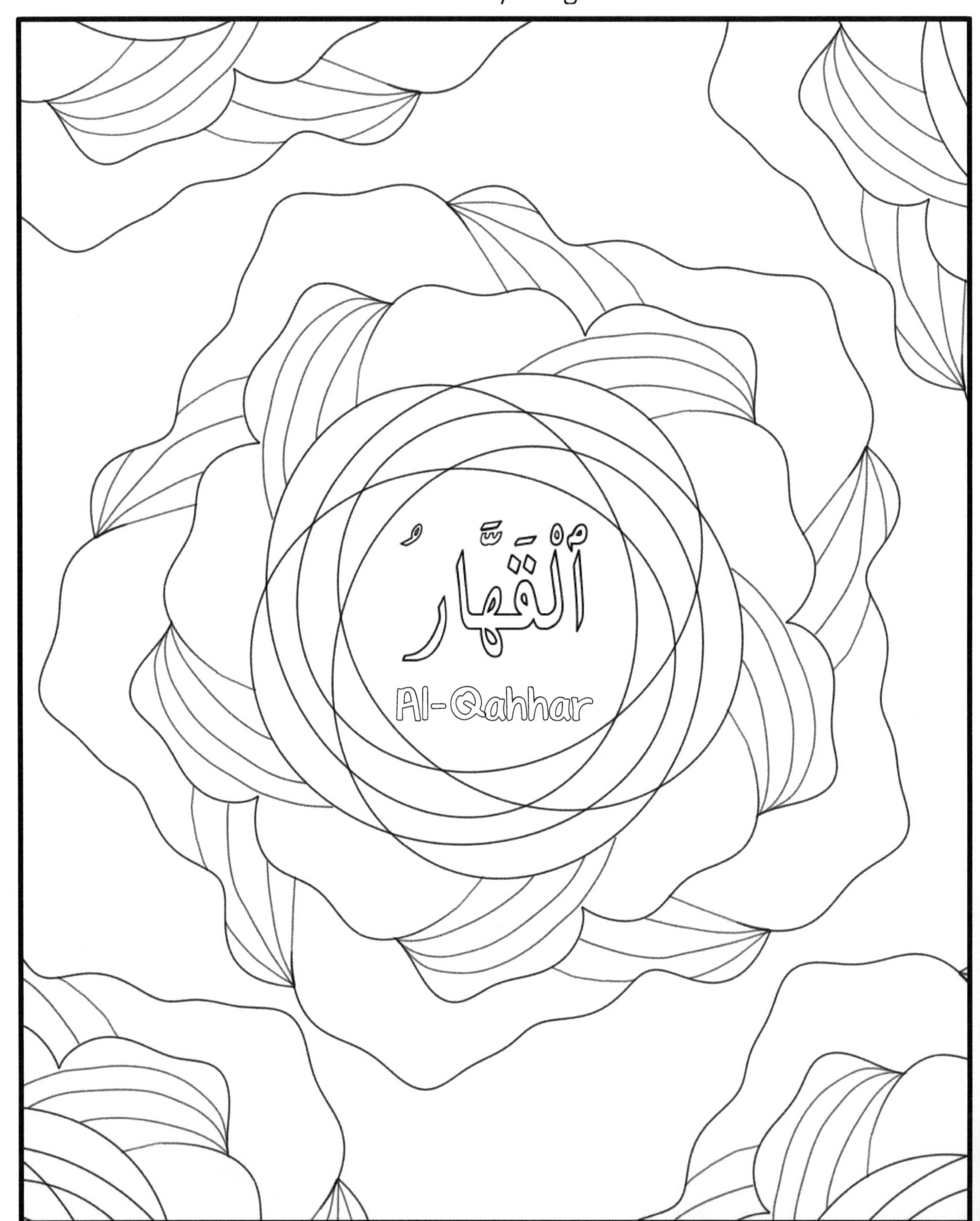

The Bestower

The One who is Generous in giving plenty without any return

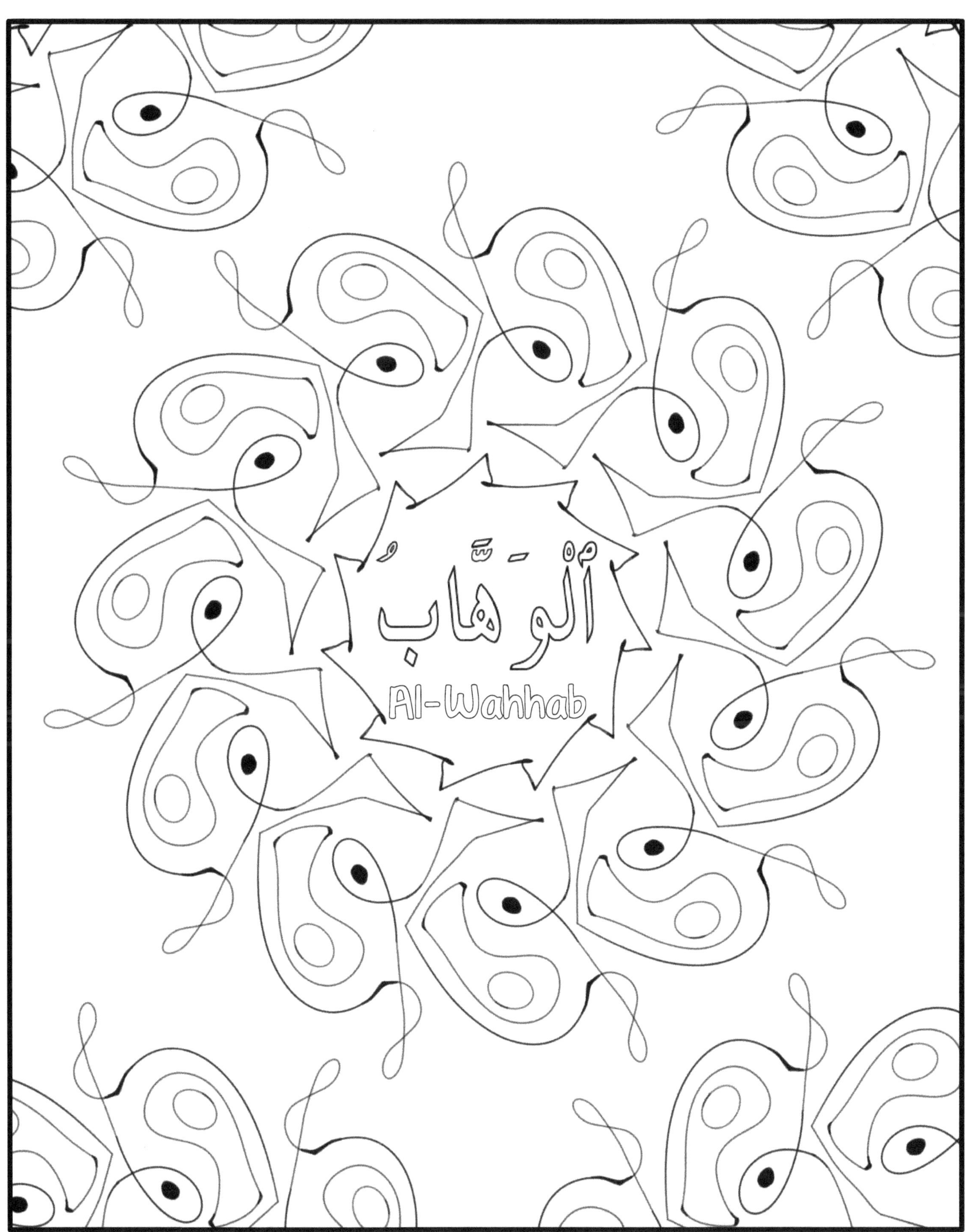

The Provider

The Sustainer, The Provider

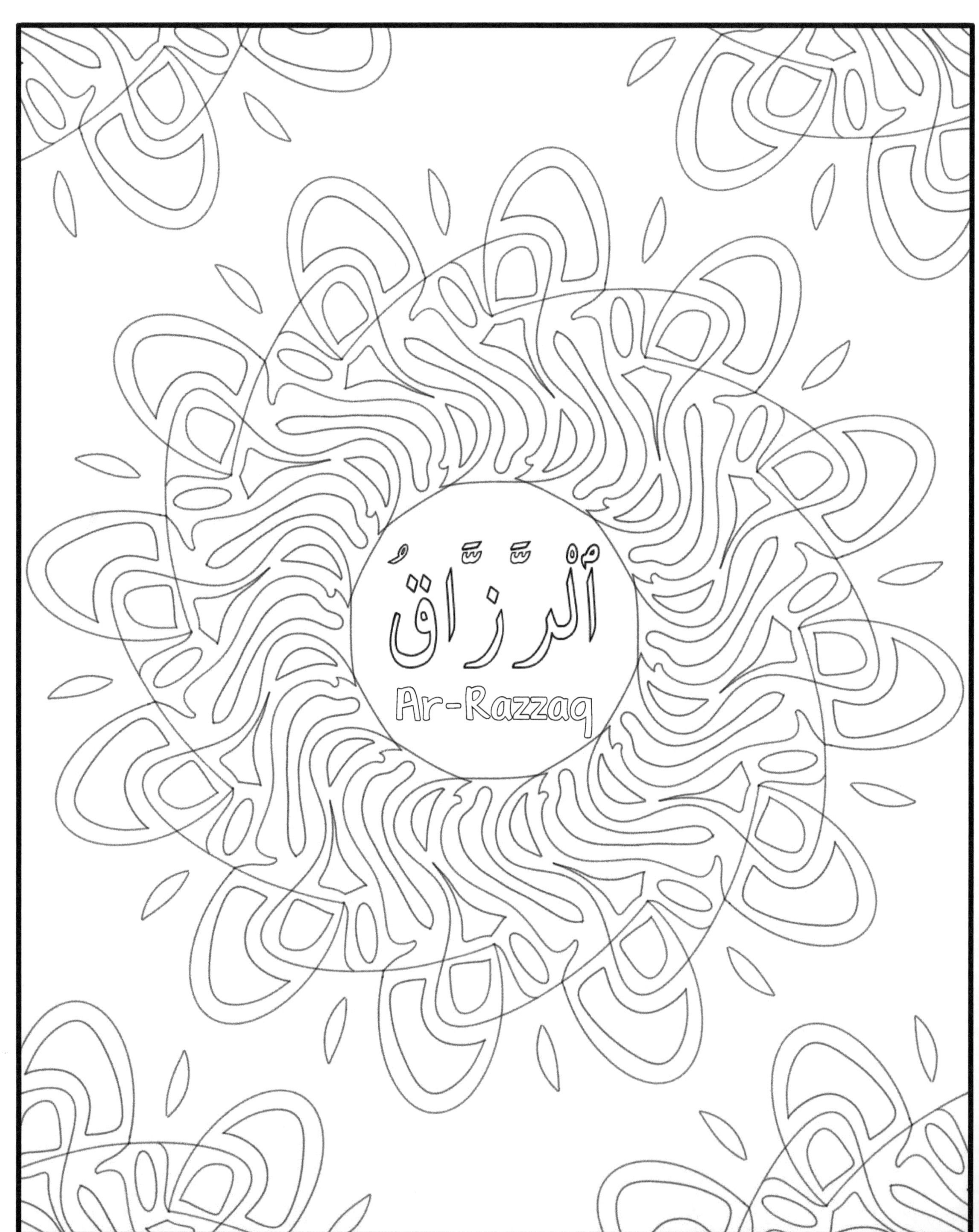

The Opener

The Solver, The Reliever, The Judge

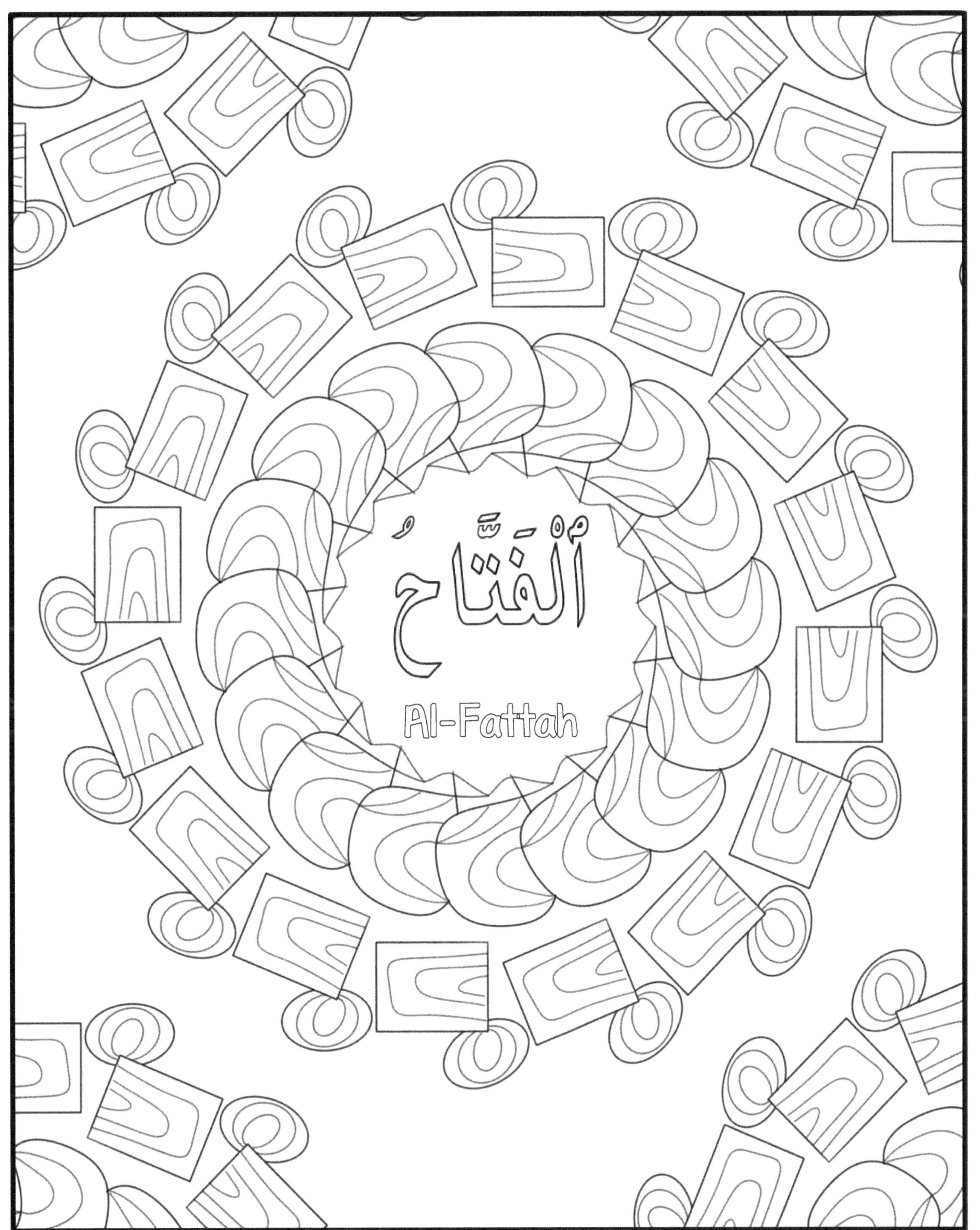

The All-Knowing

The Knowledgeable; The One nothing is absent from His knowledge

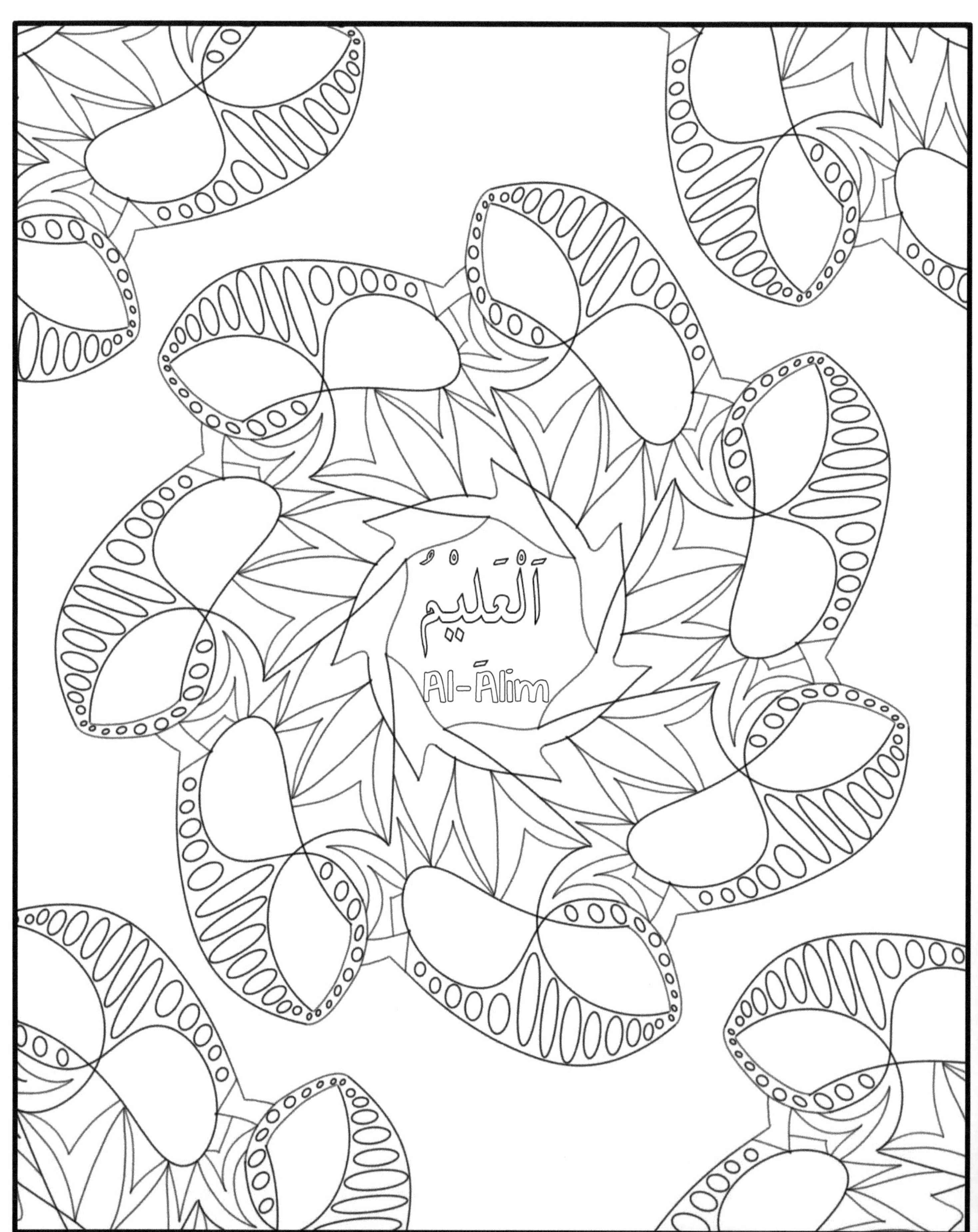

The Withholder

The Constrictor, The Withholder, The One who constricts the sustenance by His wisdom and expands and widens it with His Generosity.

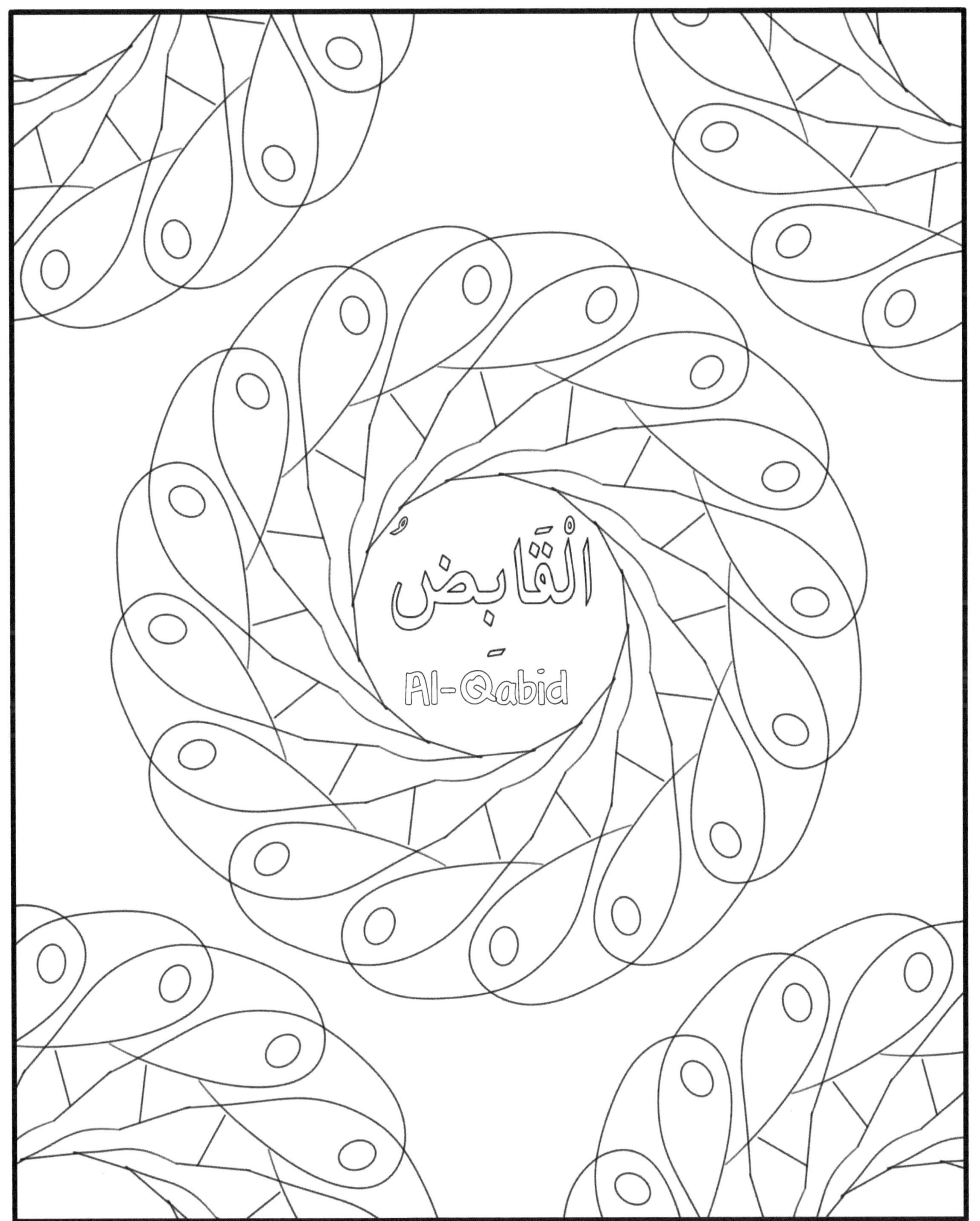

The Extender

The Enlarger, The One who constricts the sustenance by His wisdom and expands and widens it with His Generosity and Mercy.

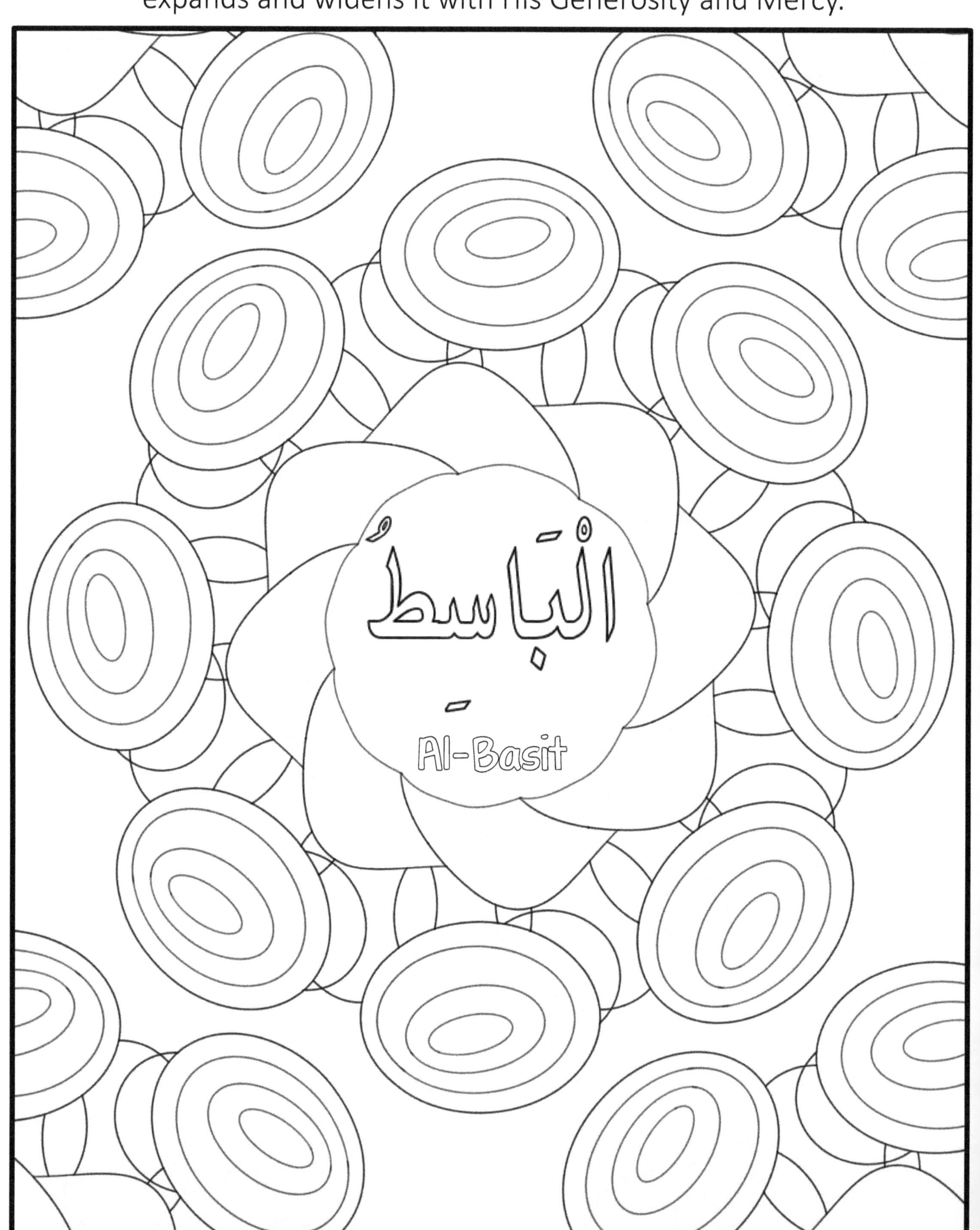

The Reducer

The Abaser, The One who lowers whoever He willed by His Destruction and raises whoever He willed by His Endowment.

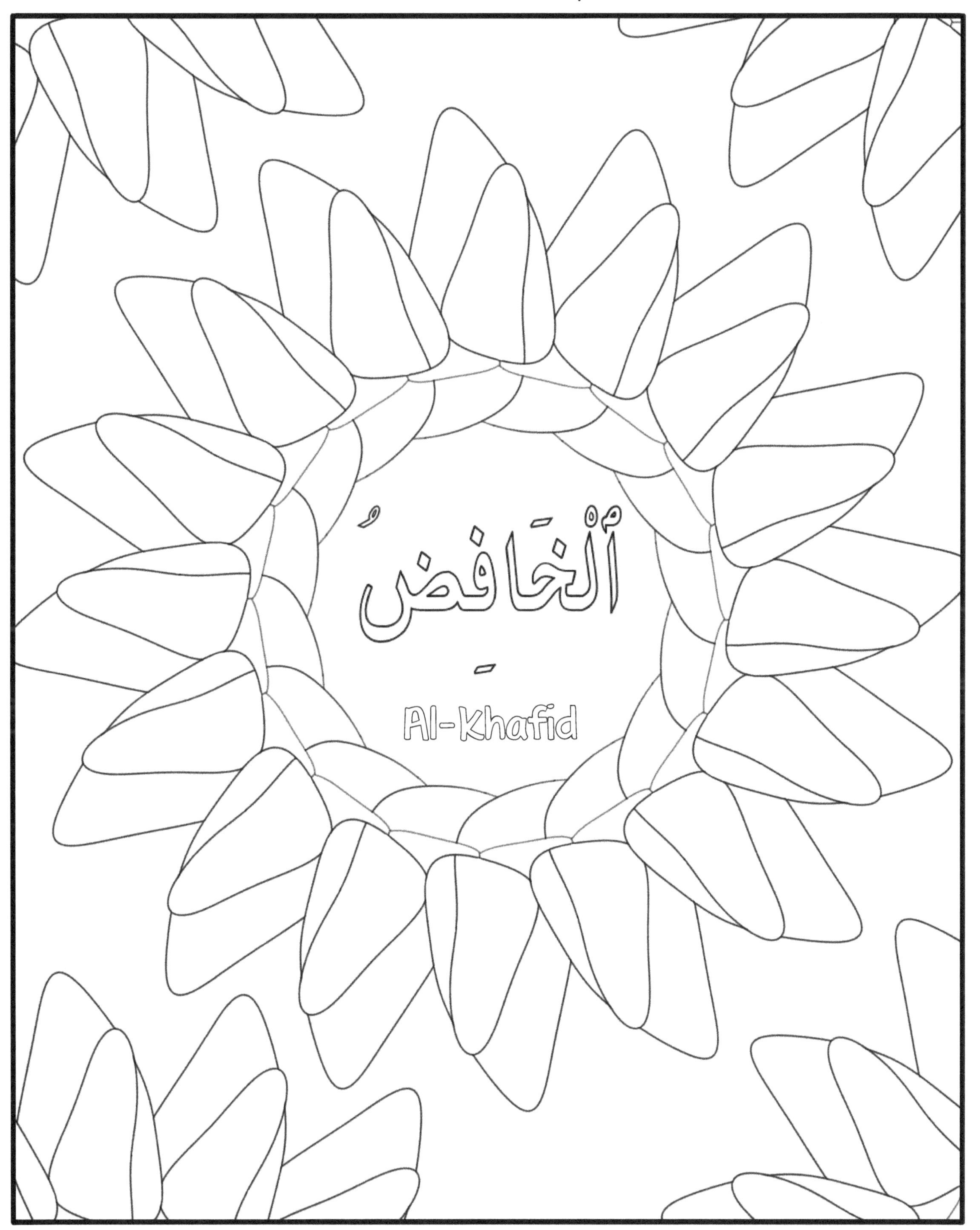

The Exalter

The Elevator, The One who lowers whoever He wills by His Destruction and raises whoever He wills by His Endowment.

The Honourer-Bestower

He gives esteem to whoever He wills, And He degrades whoever He wills.

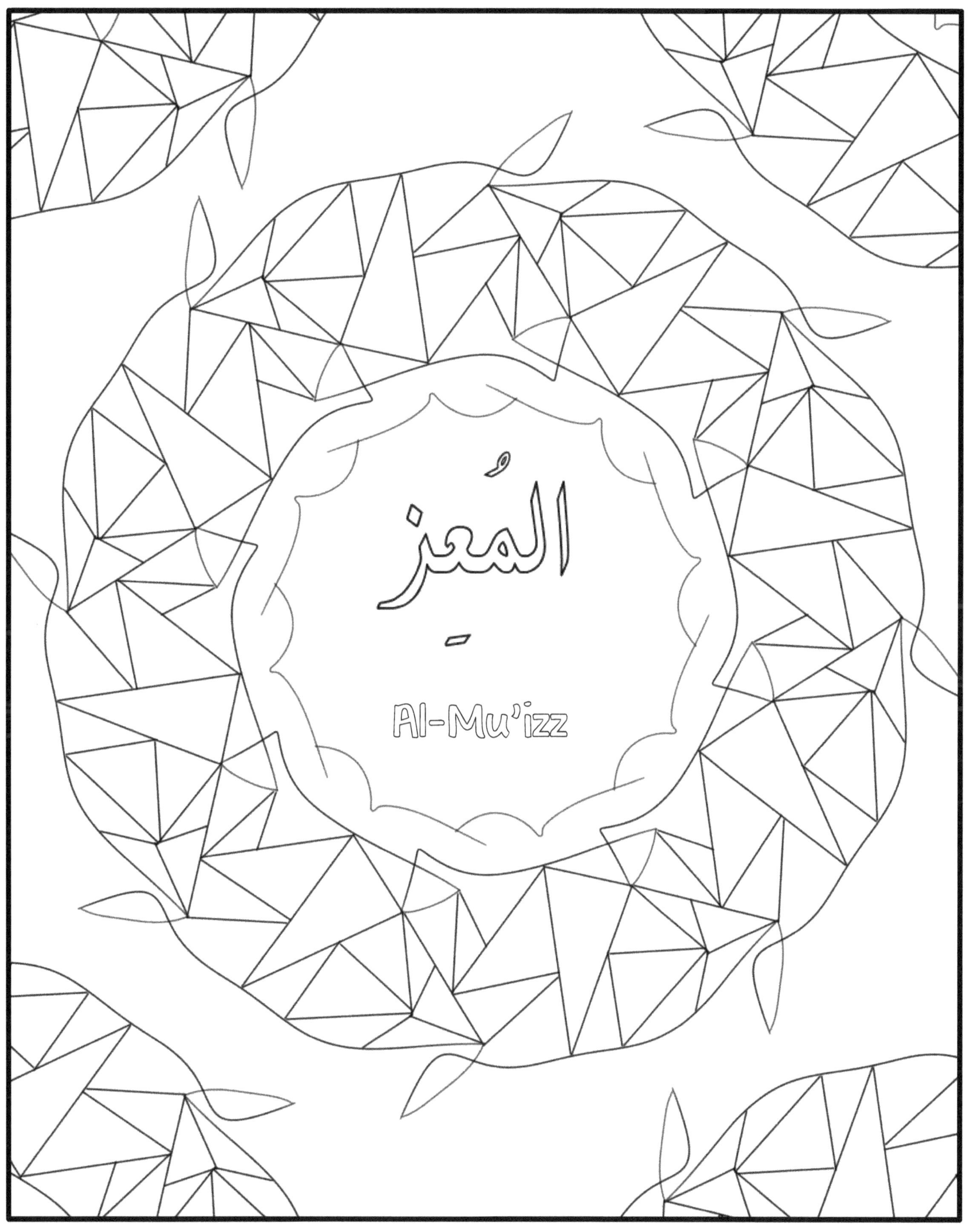

The Dishonourer

The Humiliator, He gives esteem to whoever He wills; And He degrades whoever He wills.

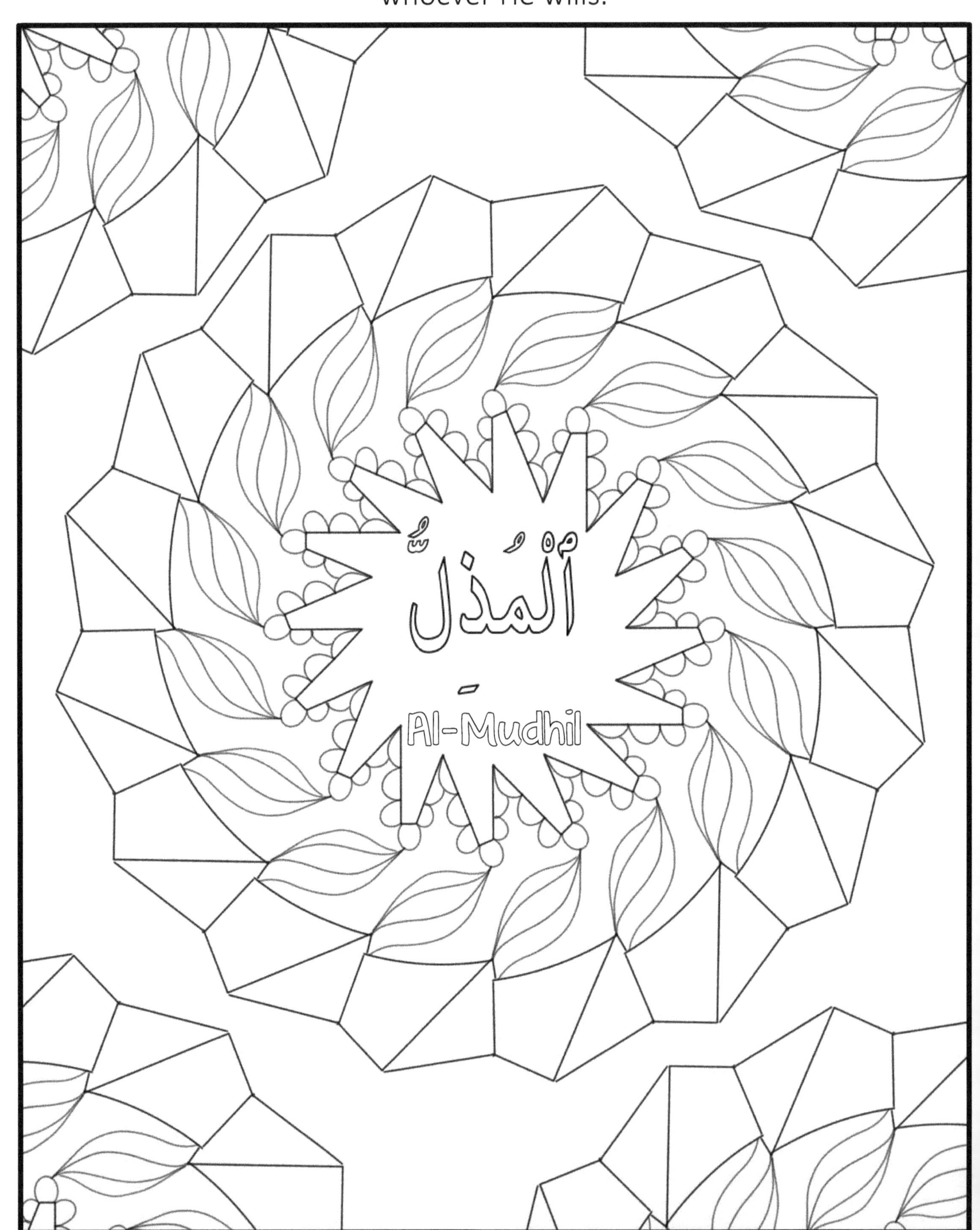

The All-Hearing

The Hearer, The One who Hears all things that are heard by His Eternal Hearing without an ear, instrument or organ.

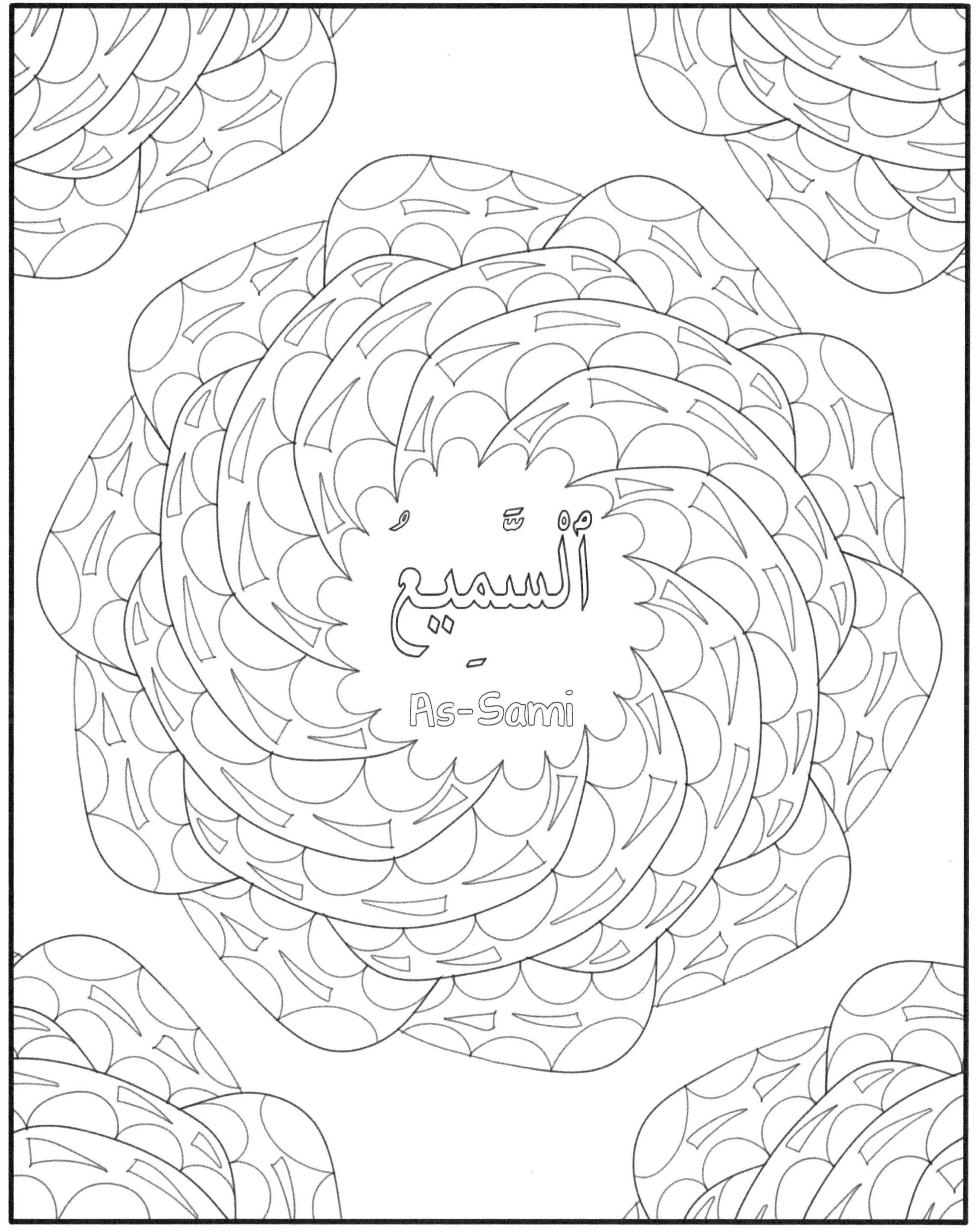

The All-Seeing

The All-Noticing, The One who Sees all things that are seen by His Eternal Seeing without a pupil or any other instrument.

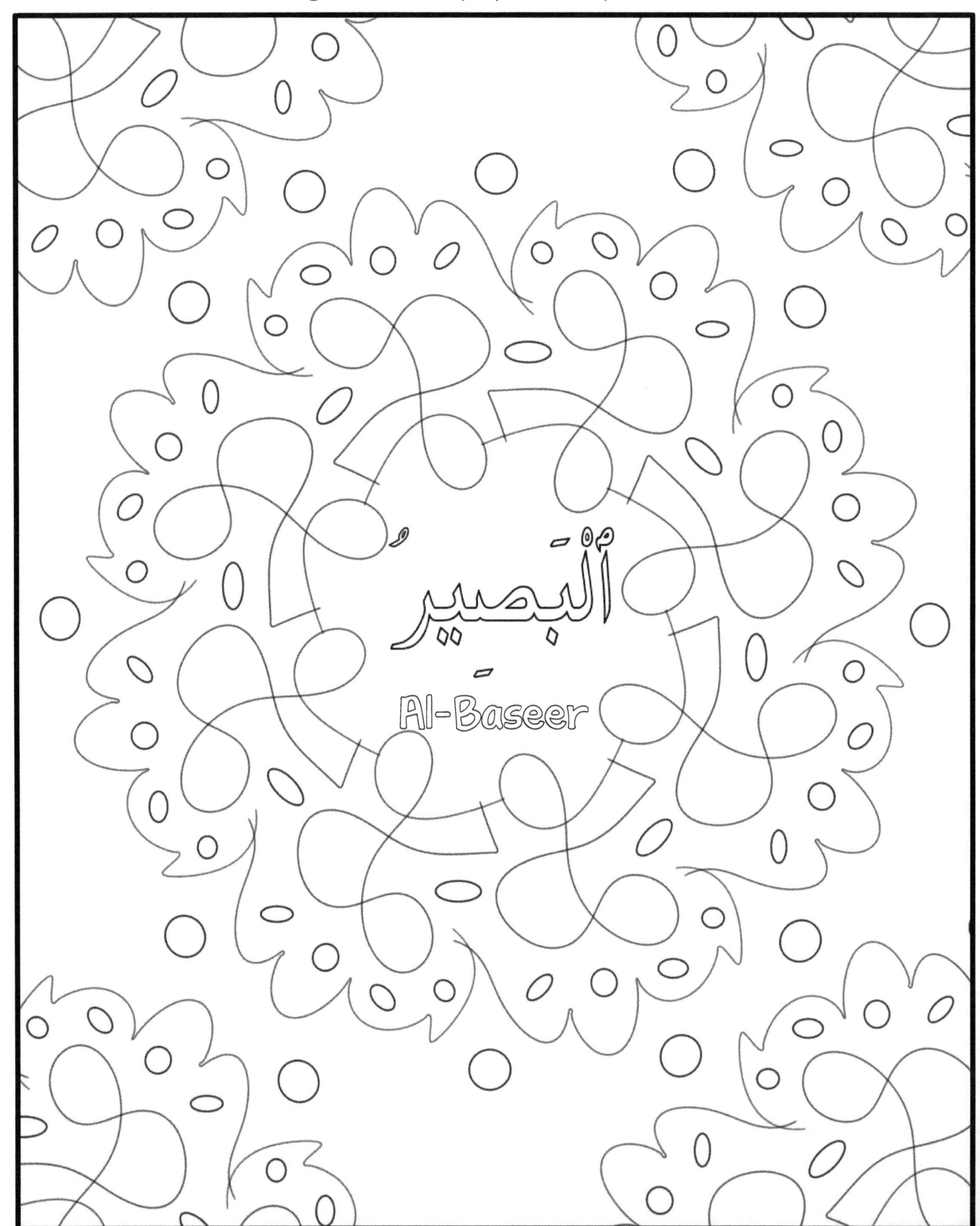

The Impartial Judge

The One who judges between His servants in this life and in the Hereafter with truth, wisdom, fairness, justice and mercy.

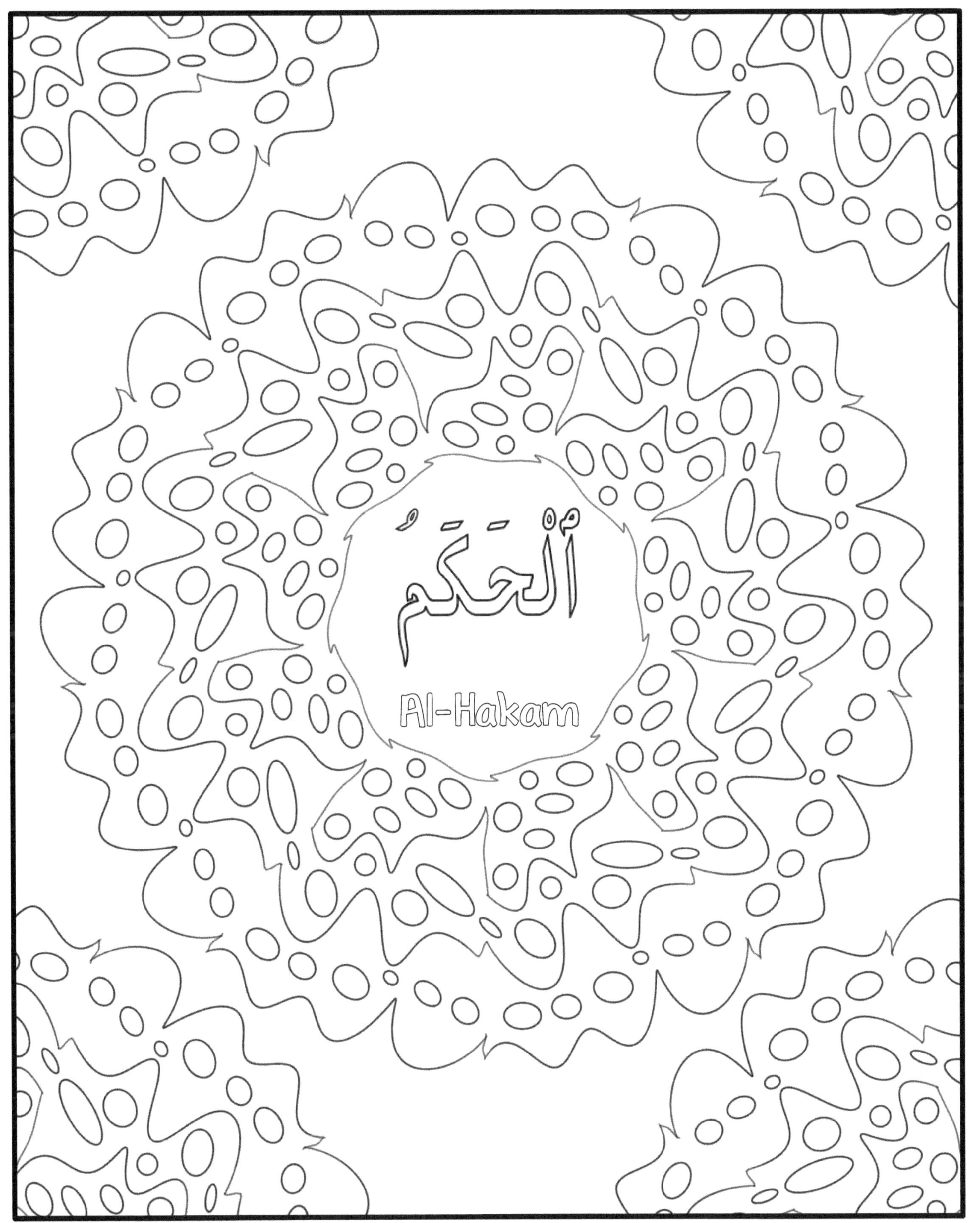

The Utterly Just

The Just, The One who is entitled to do what He does.

The Knower of Subtleties

He is aware of everything, even the subtlest details and knows what is good for His servants.

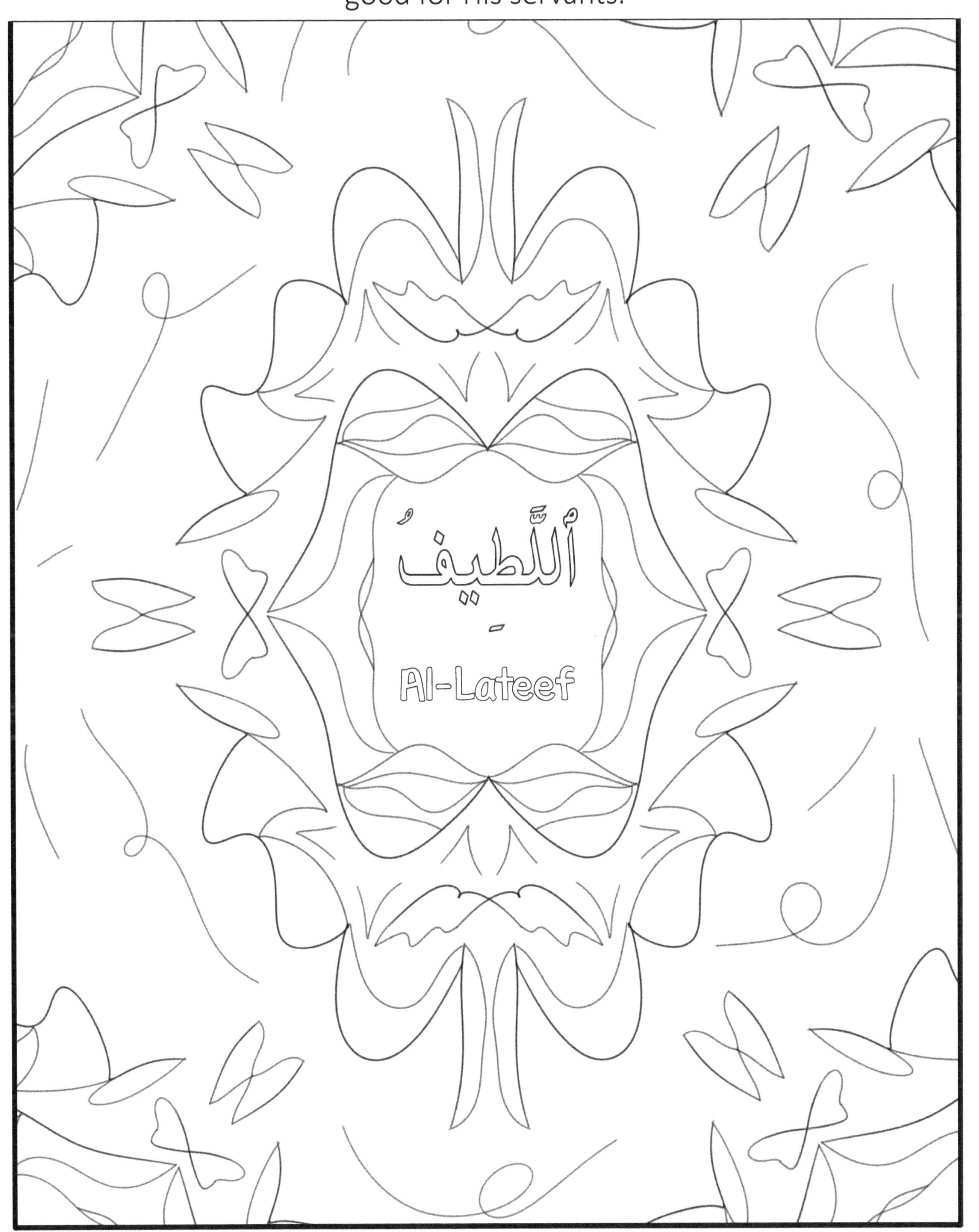

The All Aware

The One who knows what has occurred and what is still to occur.

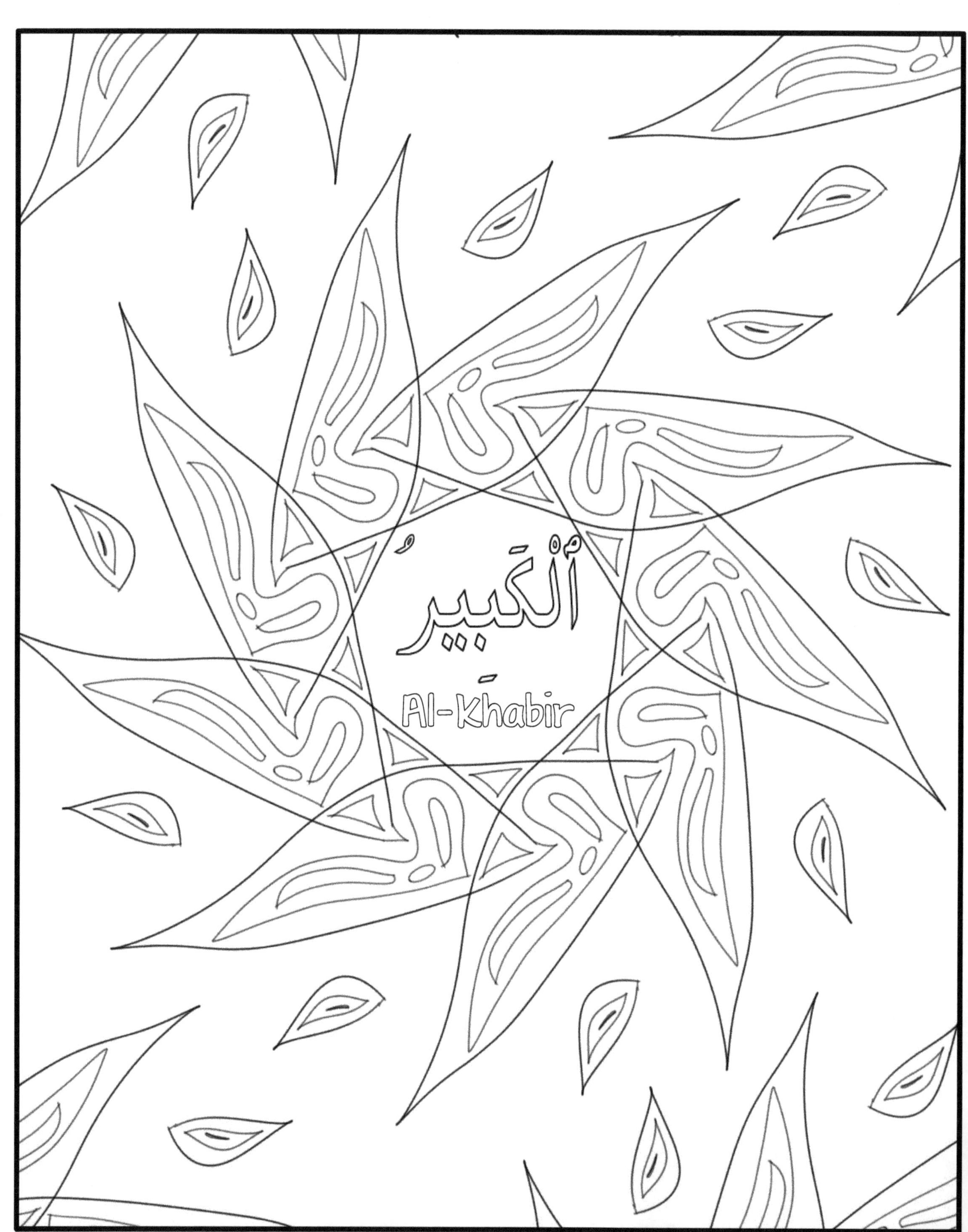

The Clement one

He is One who remains gentle and does not punish His servants for their disobedience, but rather, allows them the opportunity to repent.

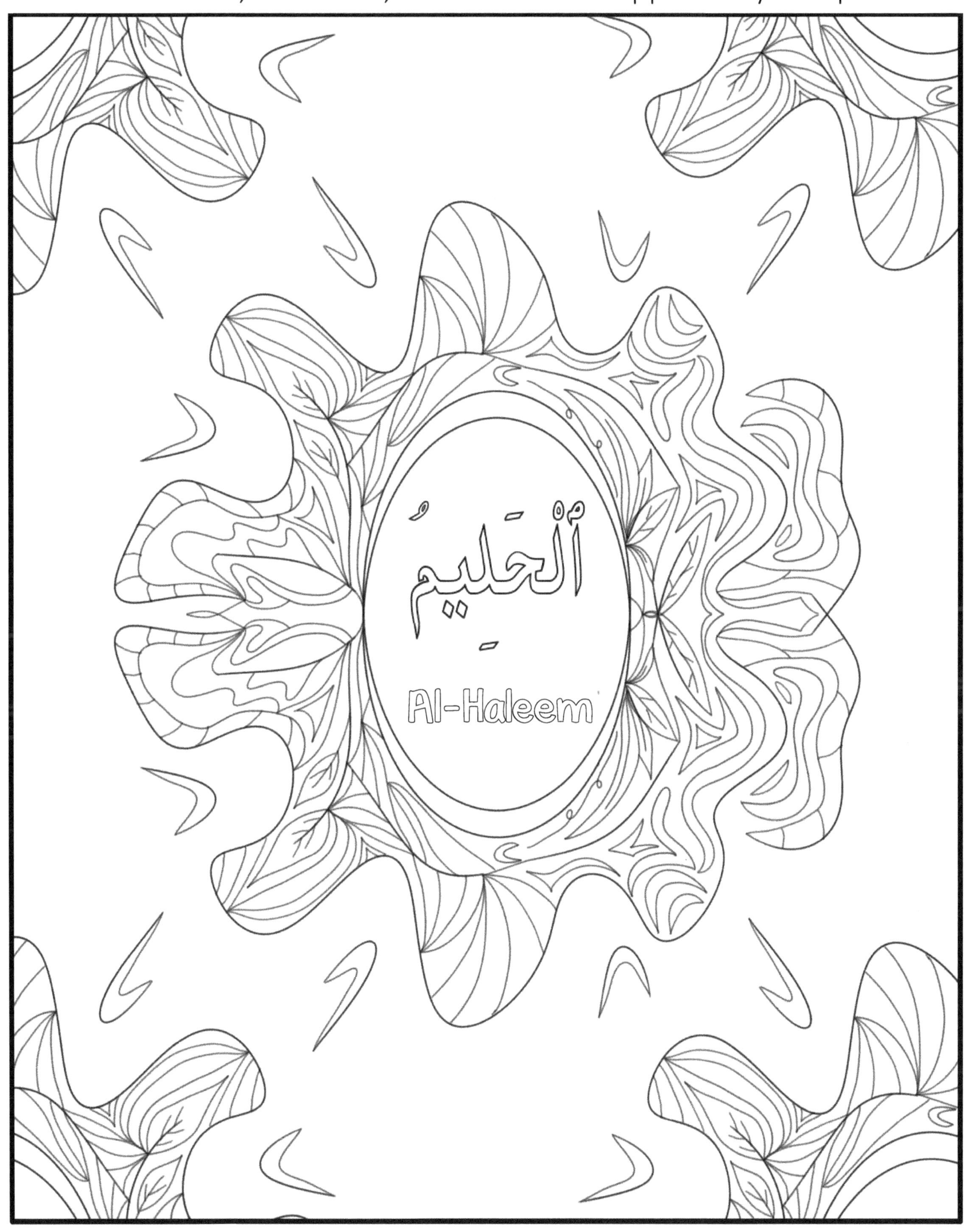

The Magnificent

The Great One, The Mighty, The One deserving the attributes of, Glory, and Purity from all imperfection.

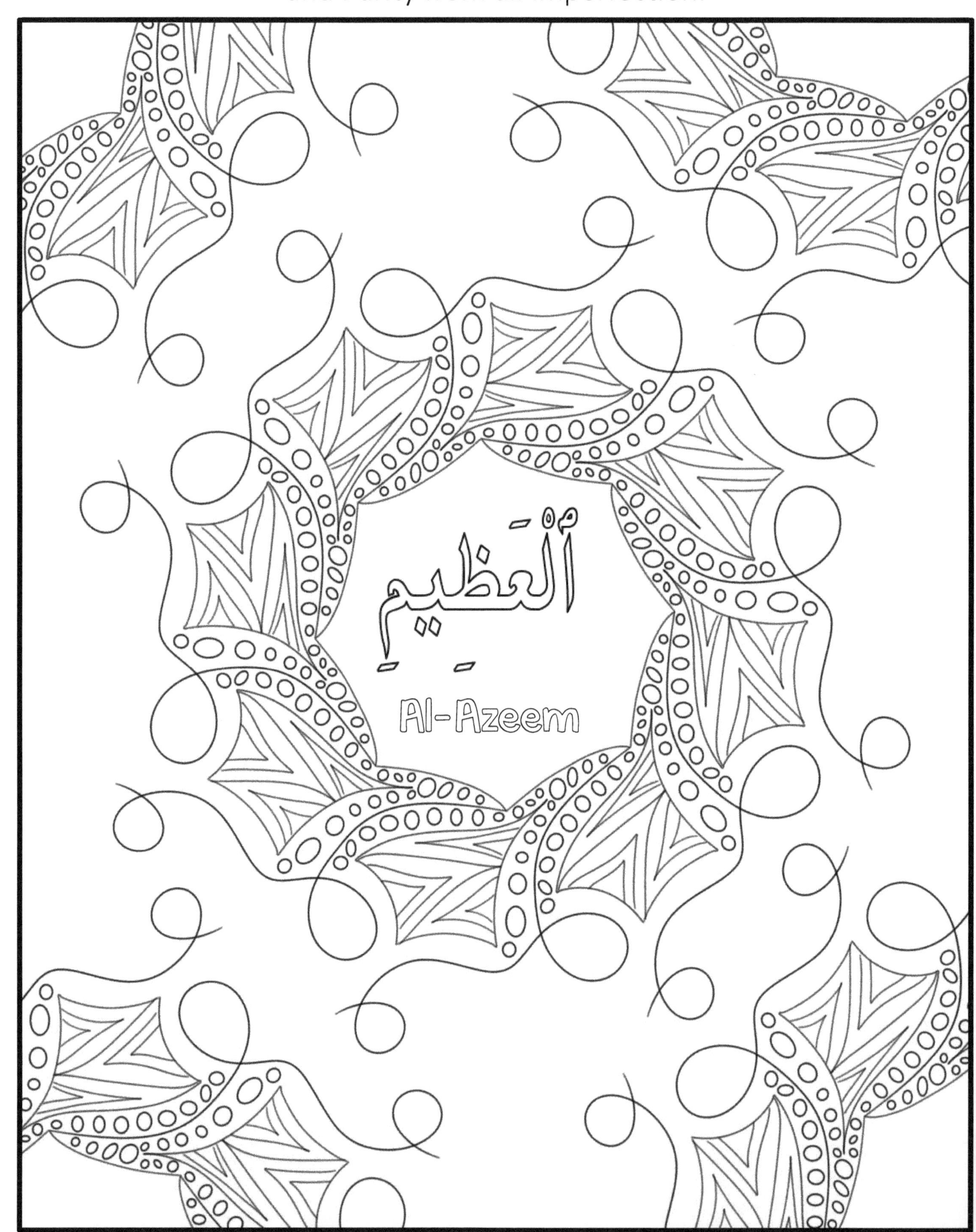

The All Forgiving

He is the One who covers up the sins of His creation. He accepts their repentance and pardons their faults.

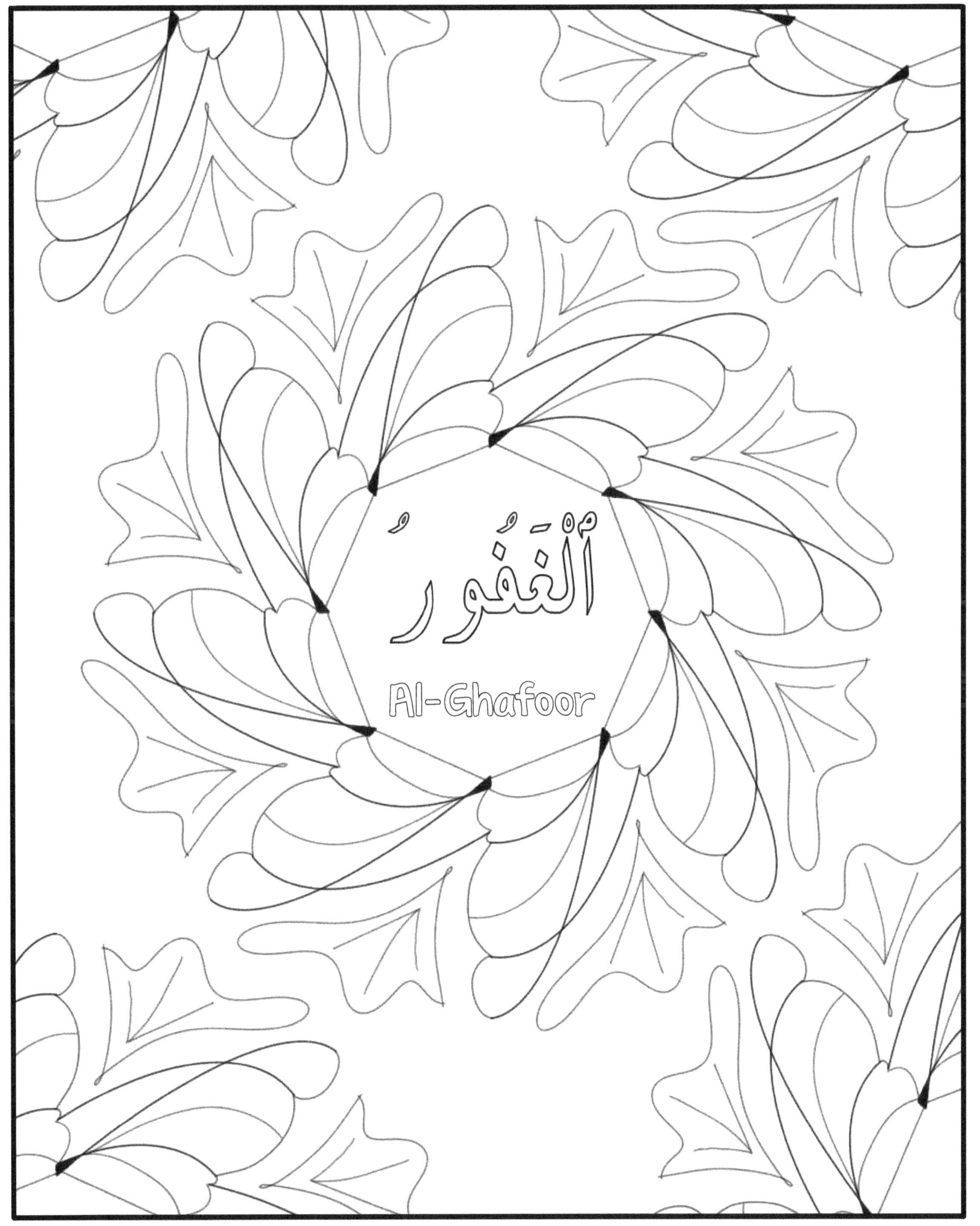

The Acknowledging One

The Grateful, The Appreciative, The One who gives a lot of reward for a little obedience.

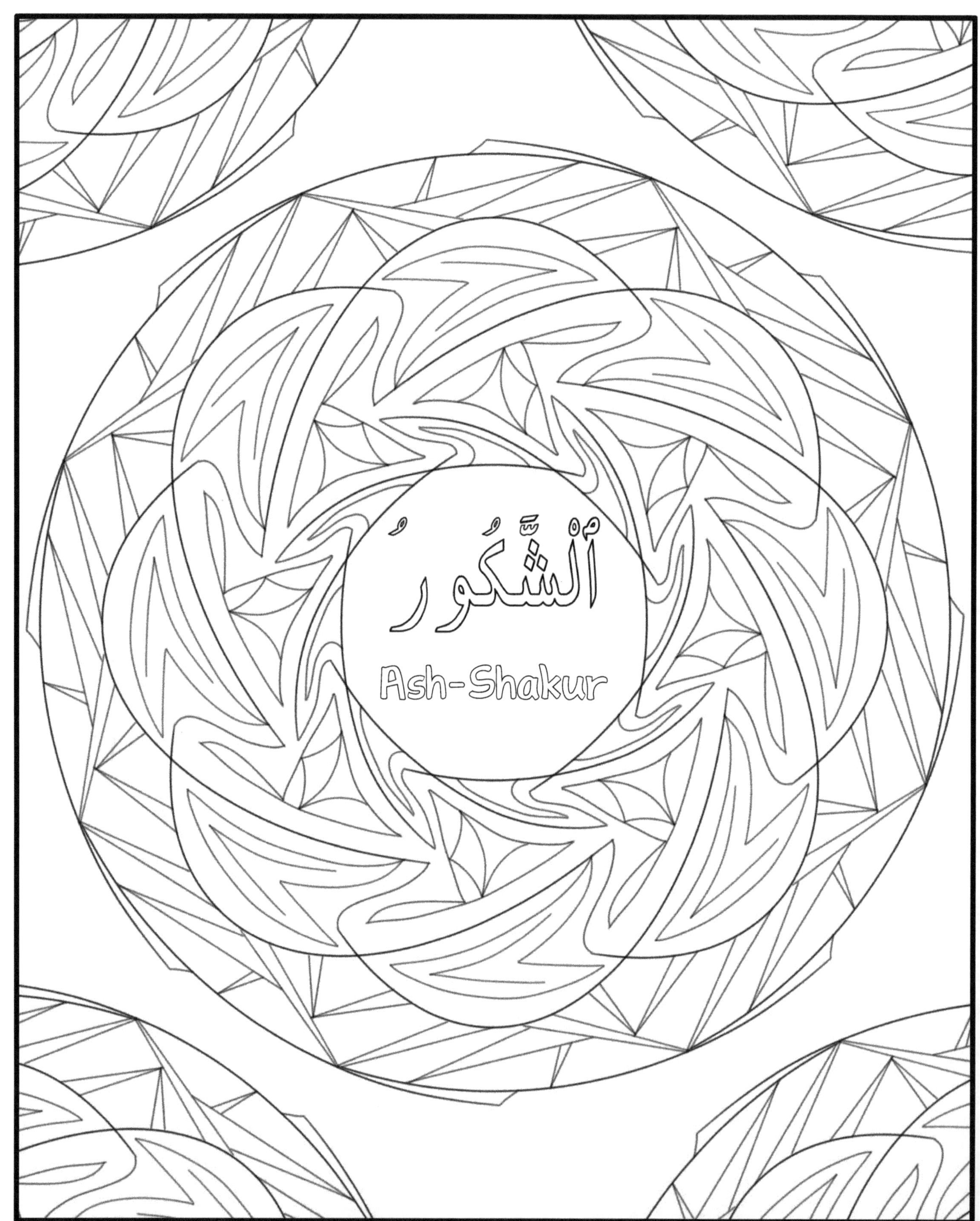

The Sublime

The Most High, The One who is clear from the attributes of the creatures.

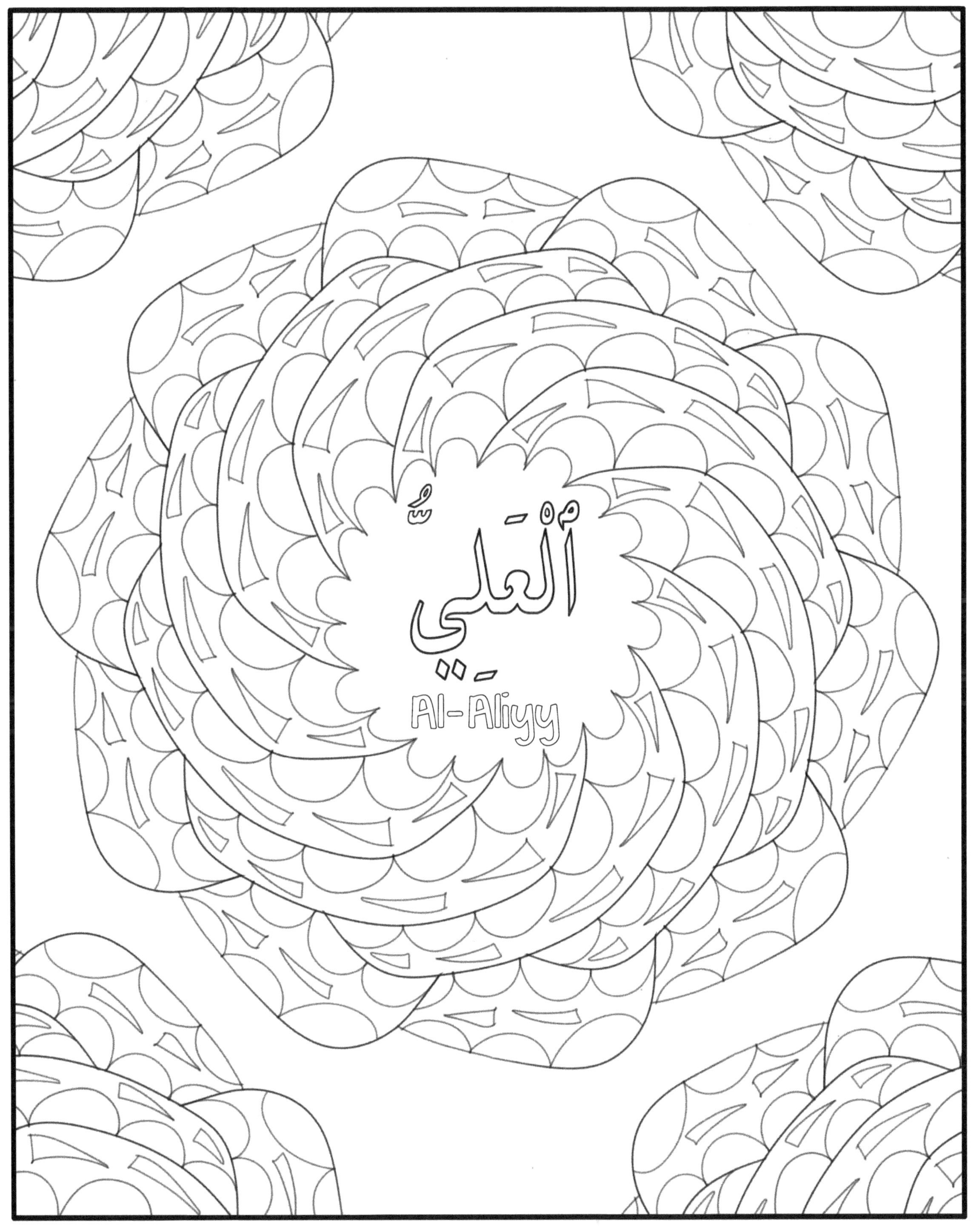

The Incomparably Great

He is greater than anything that can be imagined and everything else is insignificant before Him.

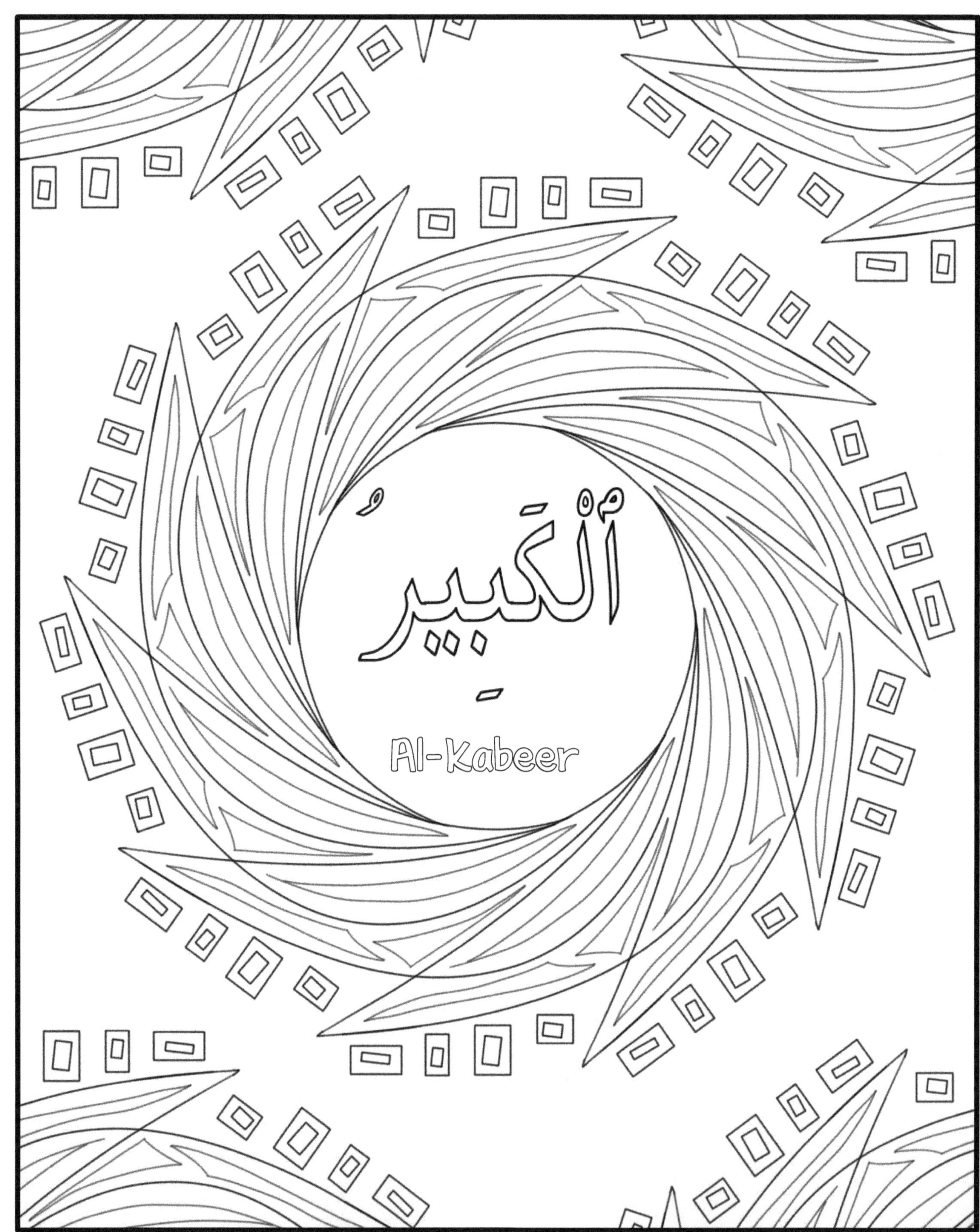

The Preserver

The One who protects and preserves all that He has created, including the deeds of His servants.

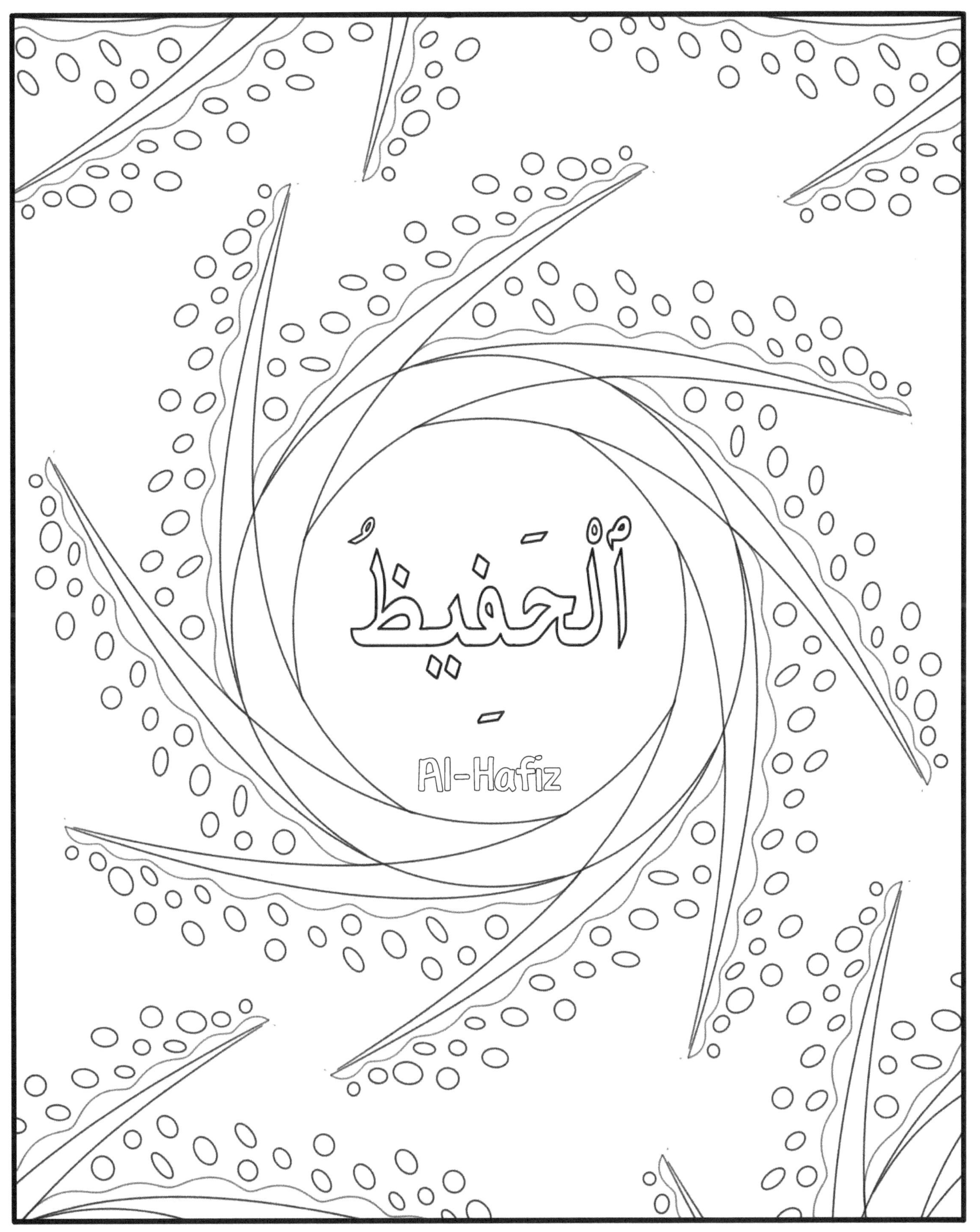

The Maintainer

He is All-Powerful who protects His creation. He provides them all they need for sustenance.

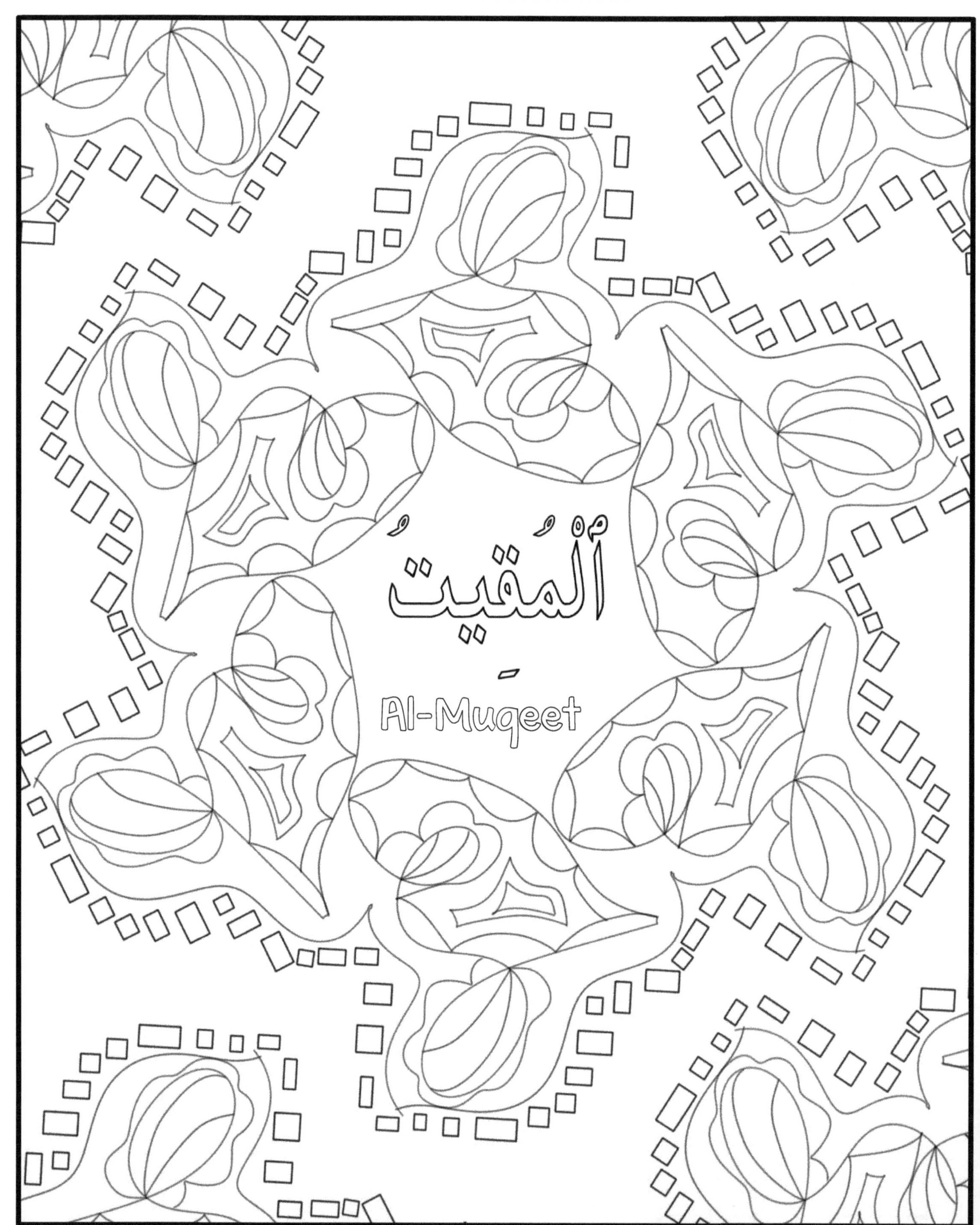

The Reckoner

The One who will take His creation to account for their deeds.

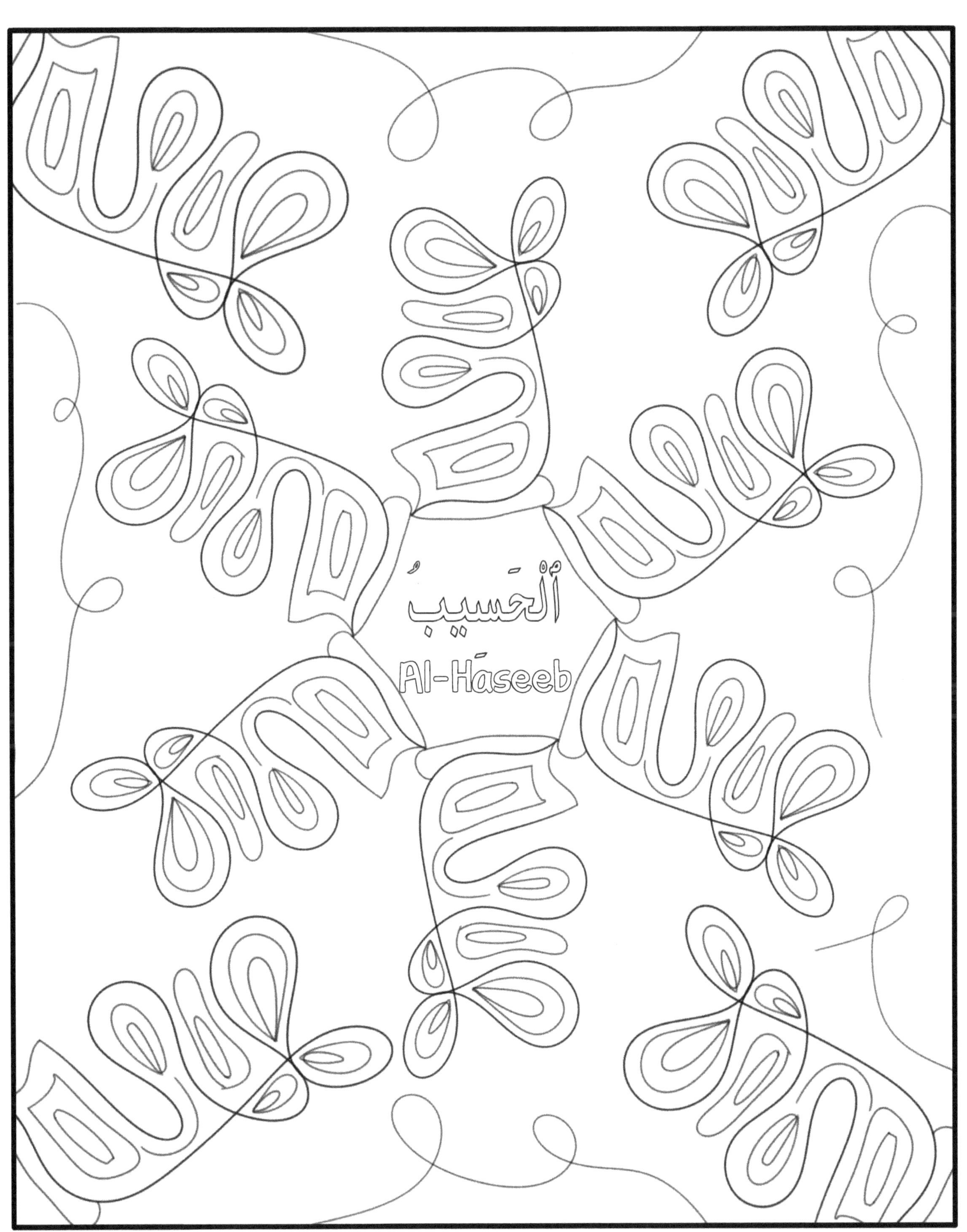

The Majestic

The One who is attributed with greatness of Power and Glory of status.

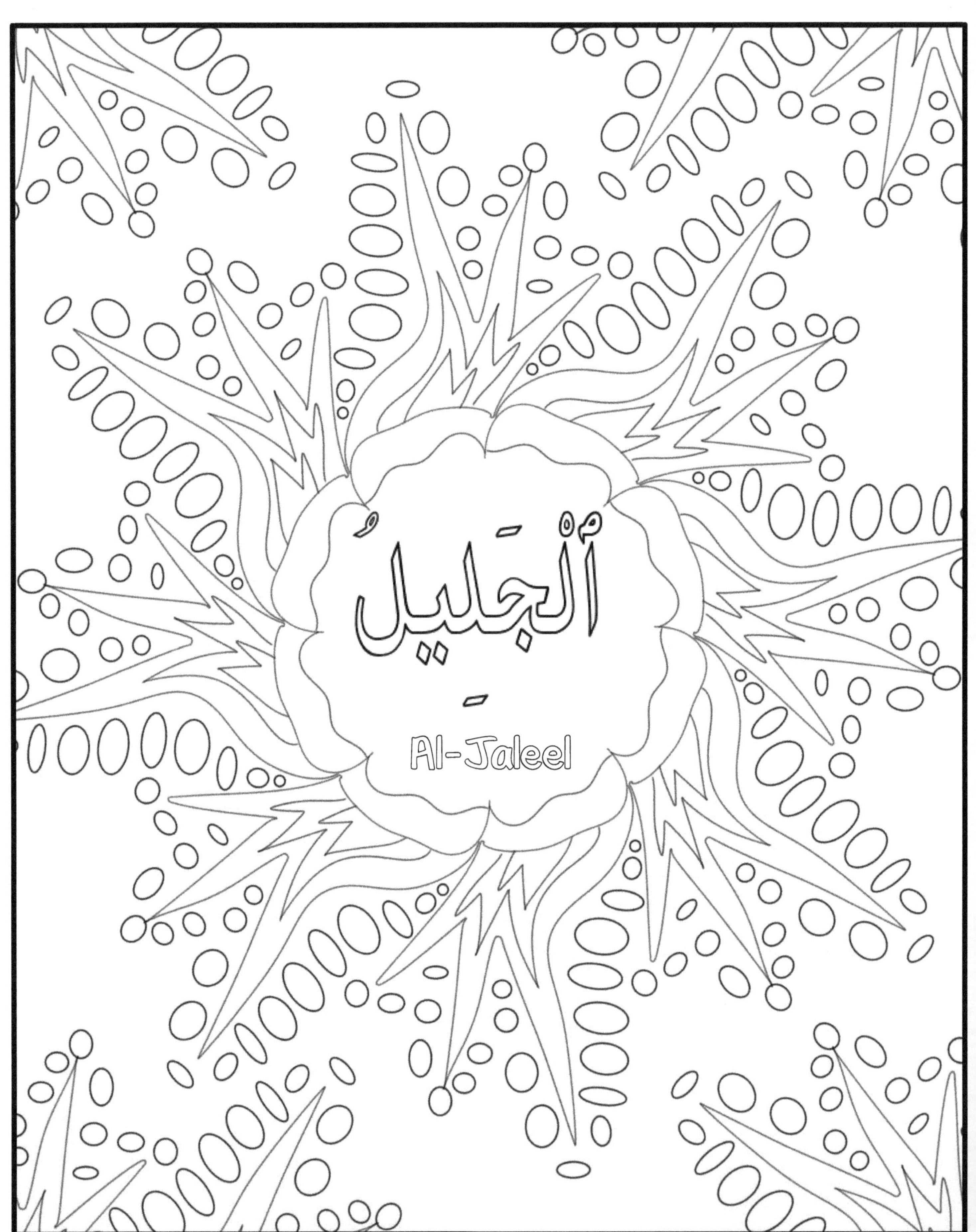

The Bountiful One

The Generous One, The Gracious, The One who is attributed with greatness of Power and Glory of status.

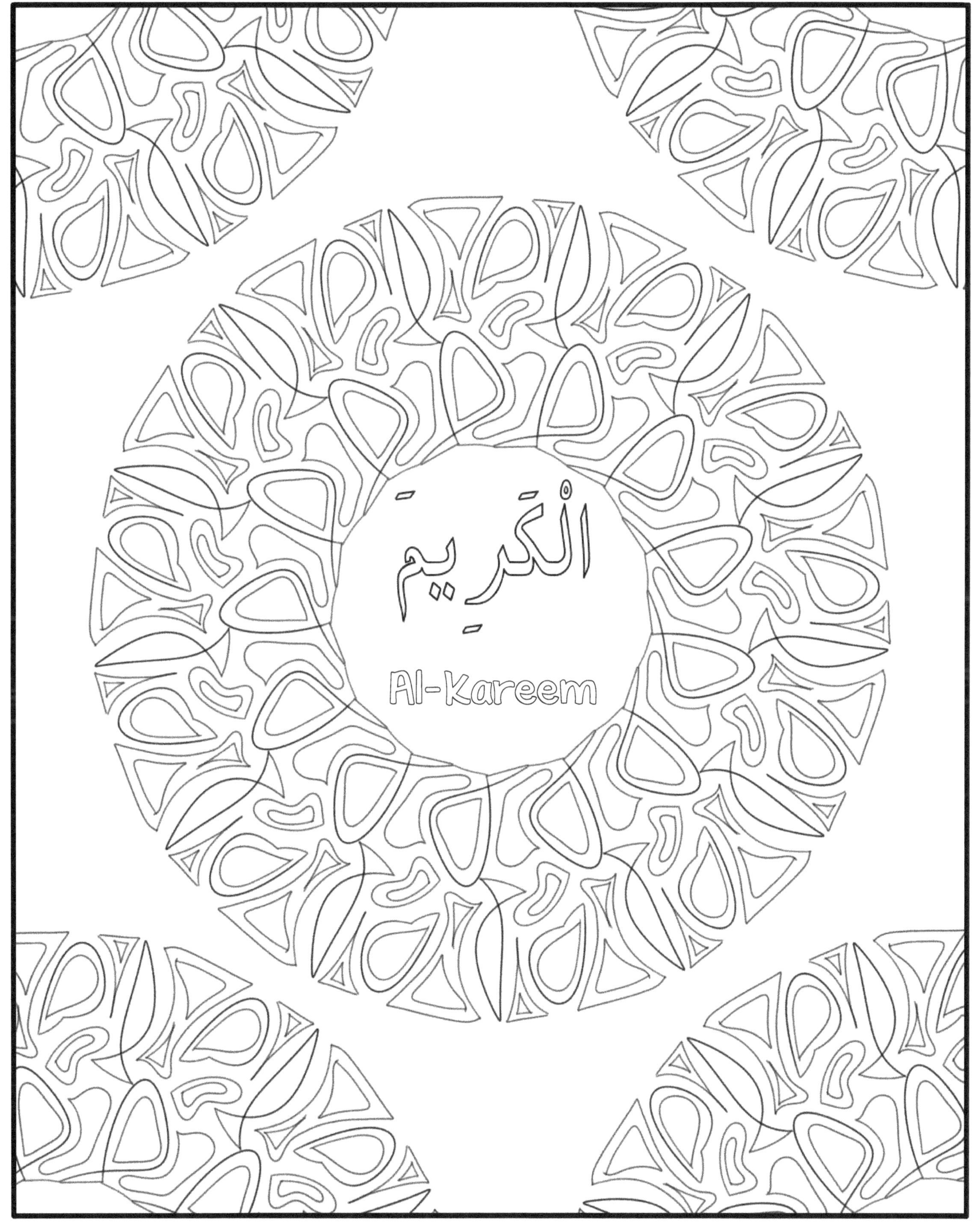

The Watchful One

The Watcher, The One that nothing is absent from Him. Hence, it's meaning is related to attribute of Knowledge

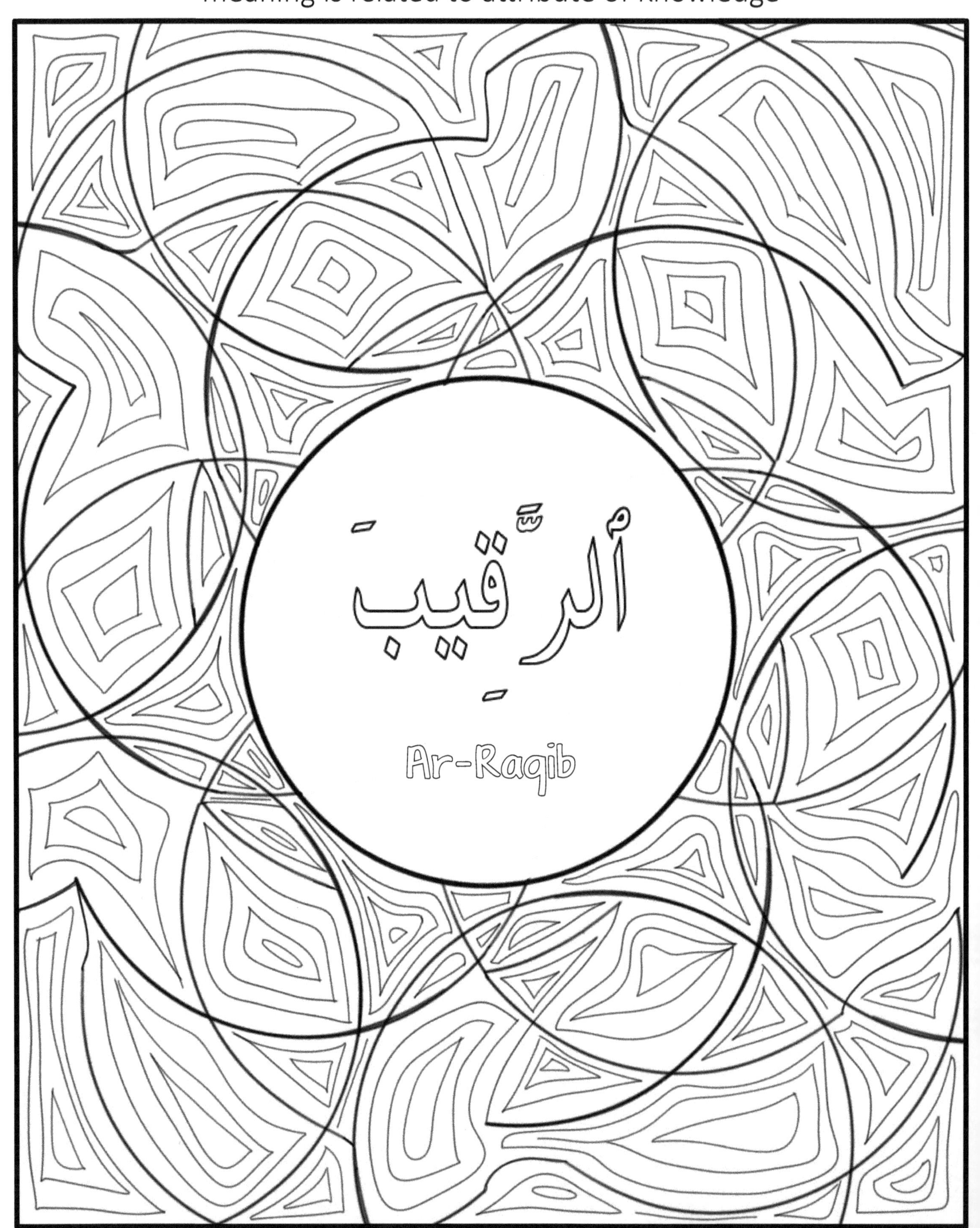

The Responding One

The Responsive, The Hearkener, The One who answers the one in need if he asks Him and rescues the yearned if he calls upon Him.

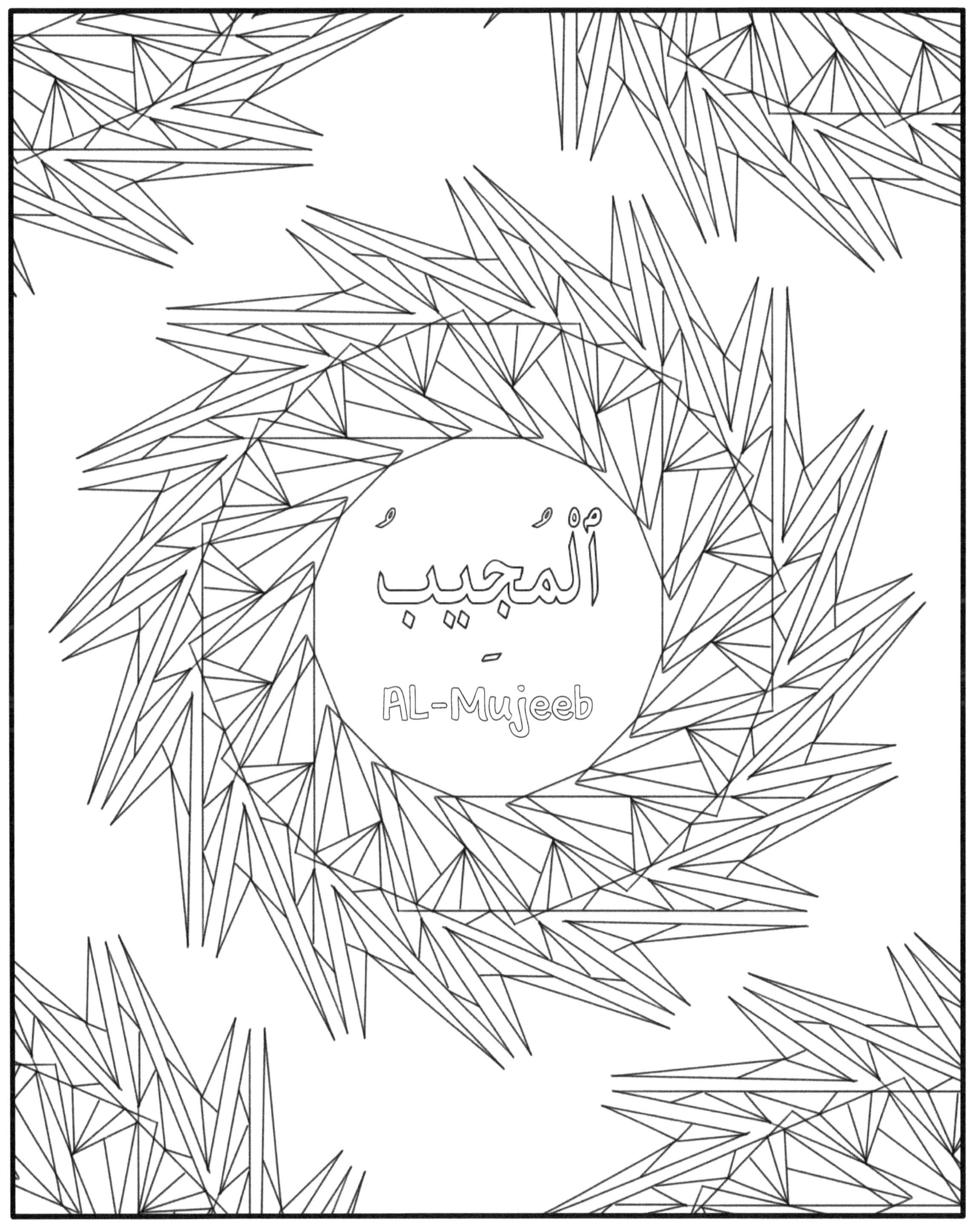

The All-Pervading

The Vast, The All-Embracing, The Knowledgeable.

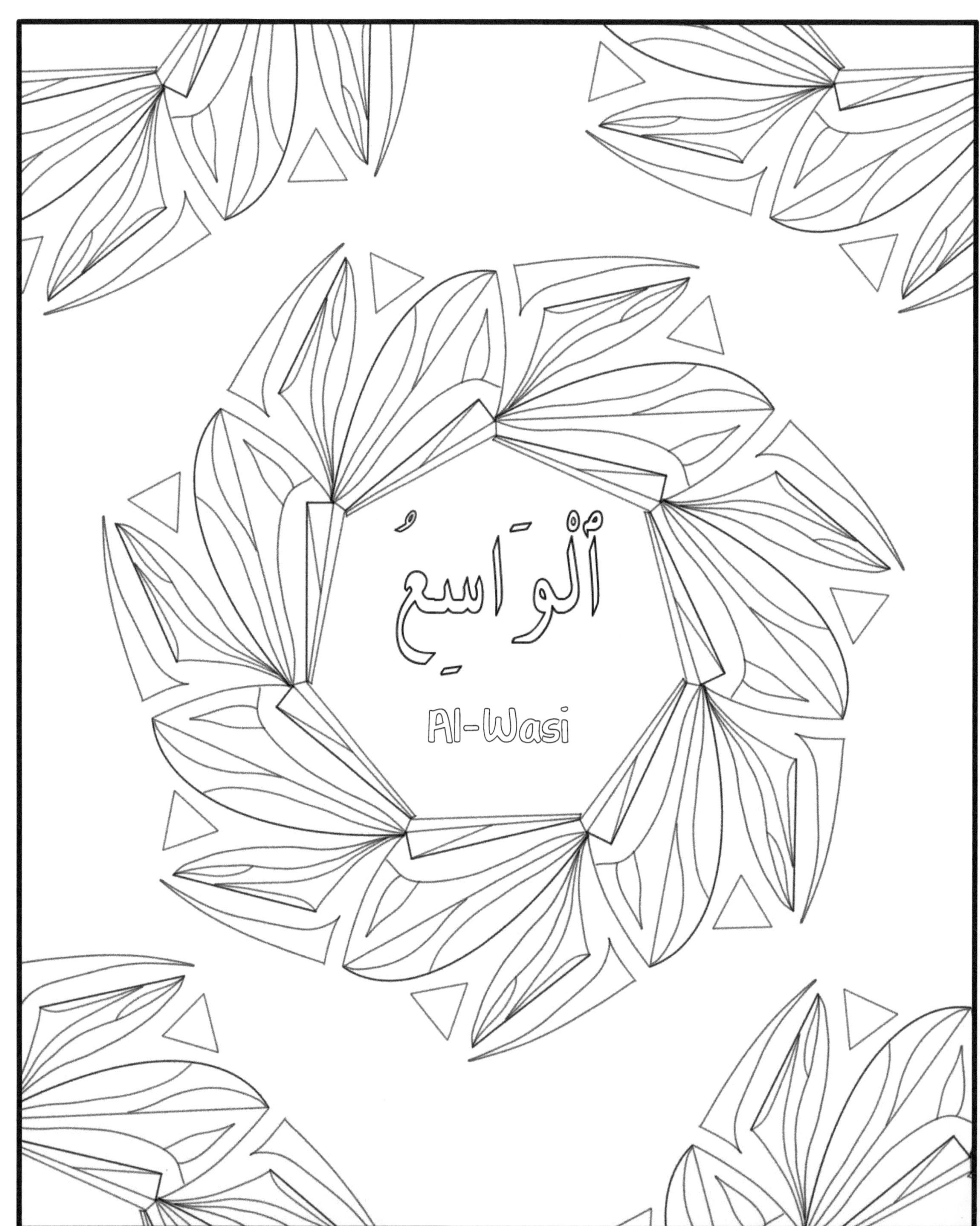

The Wise One

The Wise, The Judge of Judges, The One who is correct in His doings.

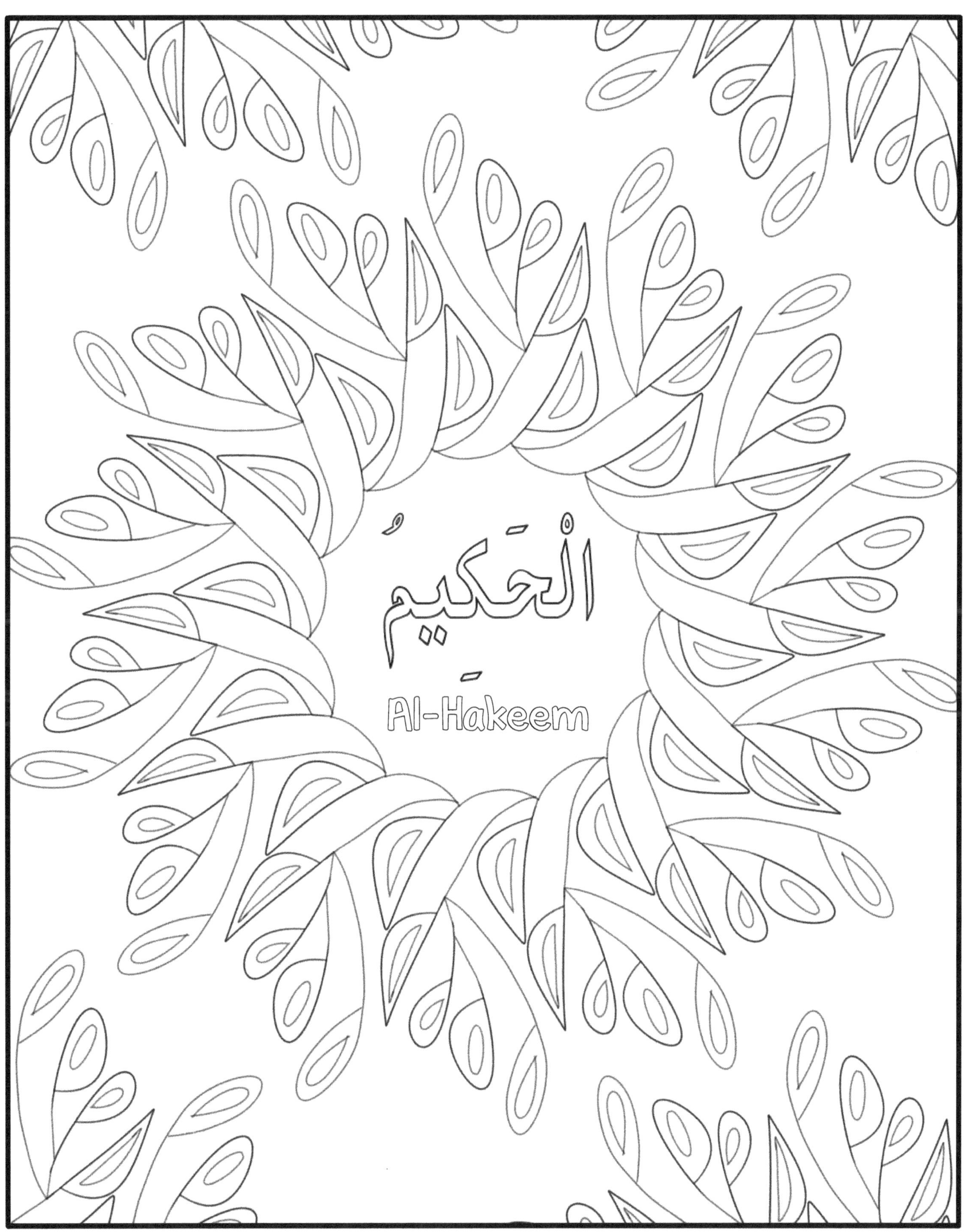

The Loving One

The Most Loving, The Most Affectionate, The Beloved

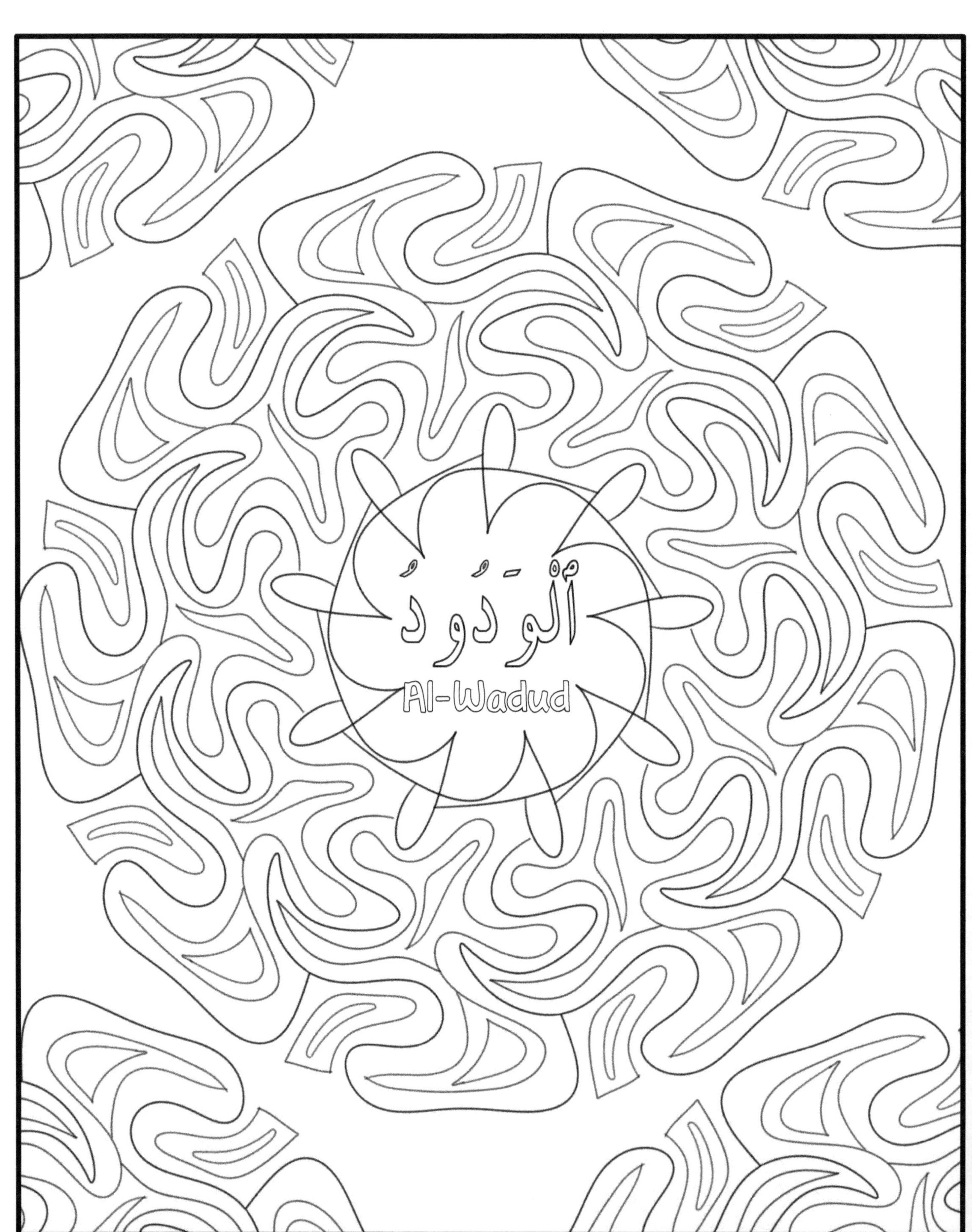

The Glorious One

The Most Glorious One, The One who is with perfect Power, High Status, Compassion, Generosity and Kindness.

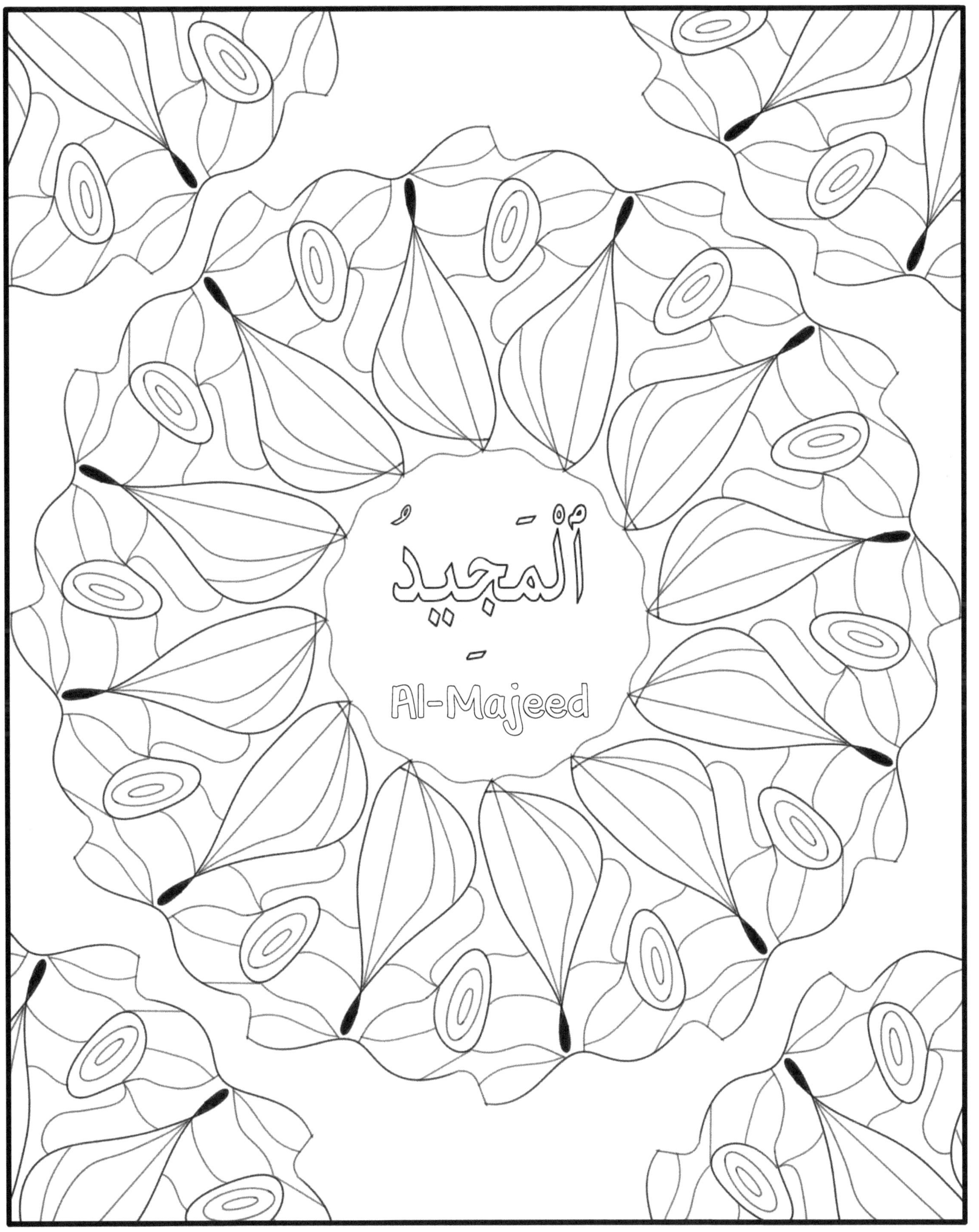

The Infuser of New Life

The Awakener, The Resurrector, The Arouser

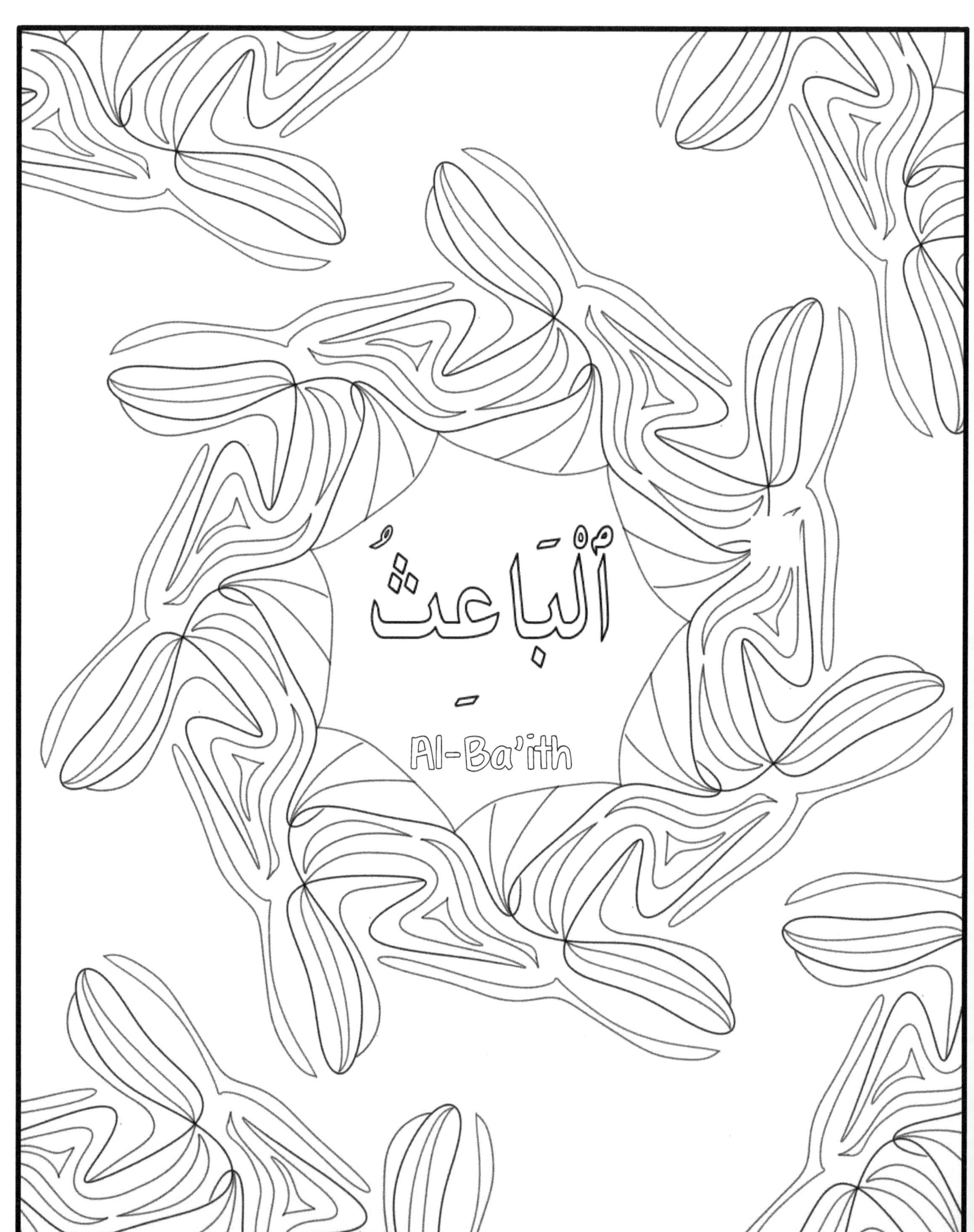

The All Observing Witness

The Witness, The One who nothing is absent from Him.

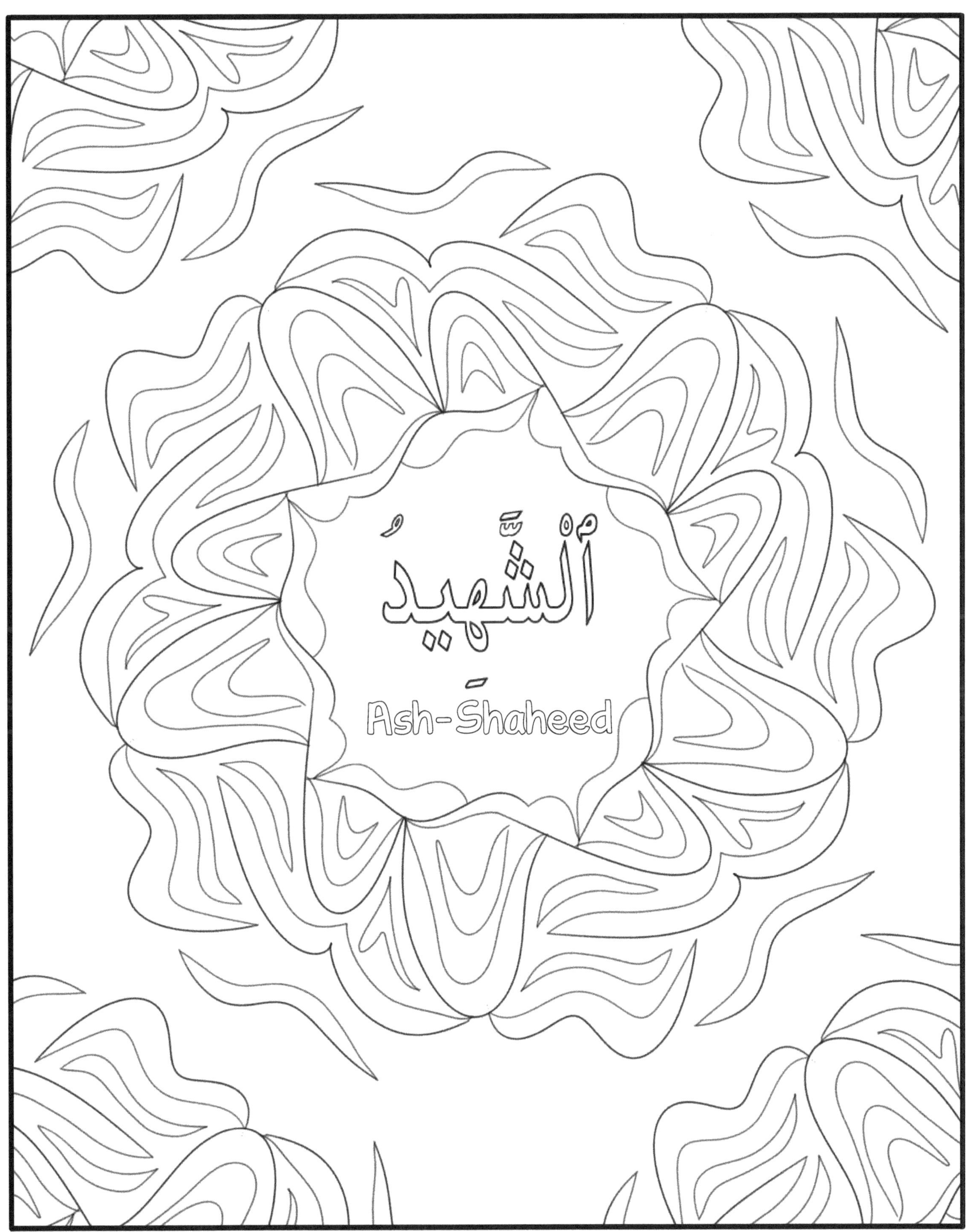

The Embodiment of Truth

The Truth, The True, The One who truly exists.

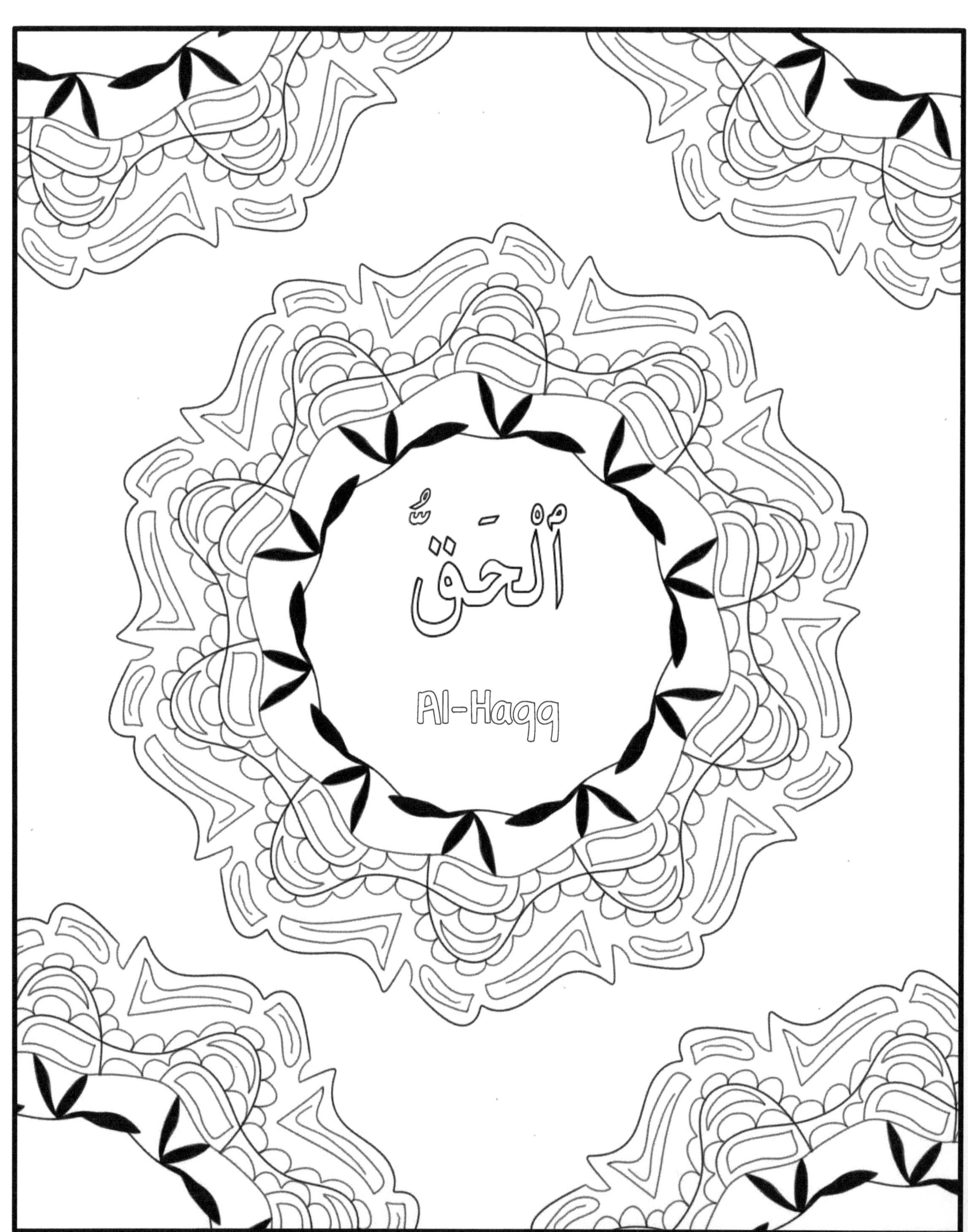

The Universal Trustee

The Trustee, The One who gives the satisfaction and is relied upon

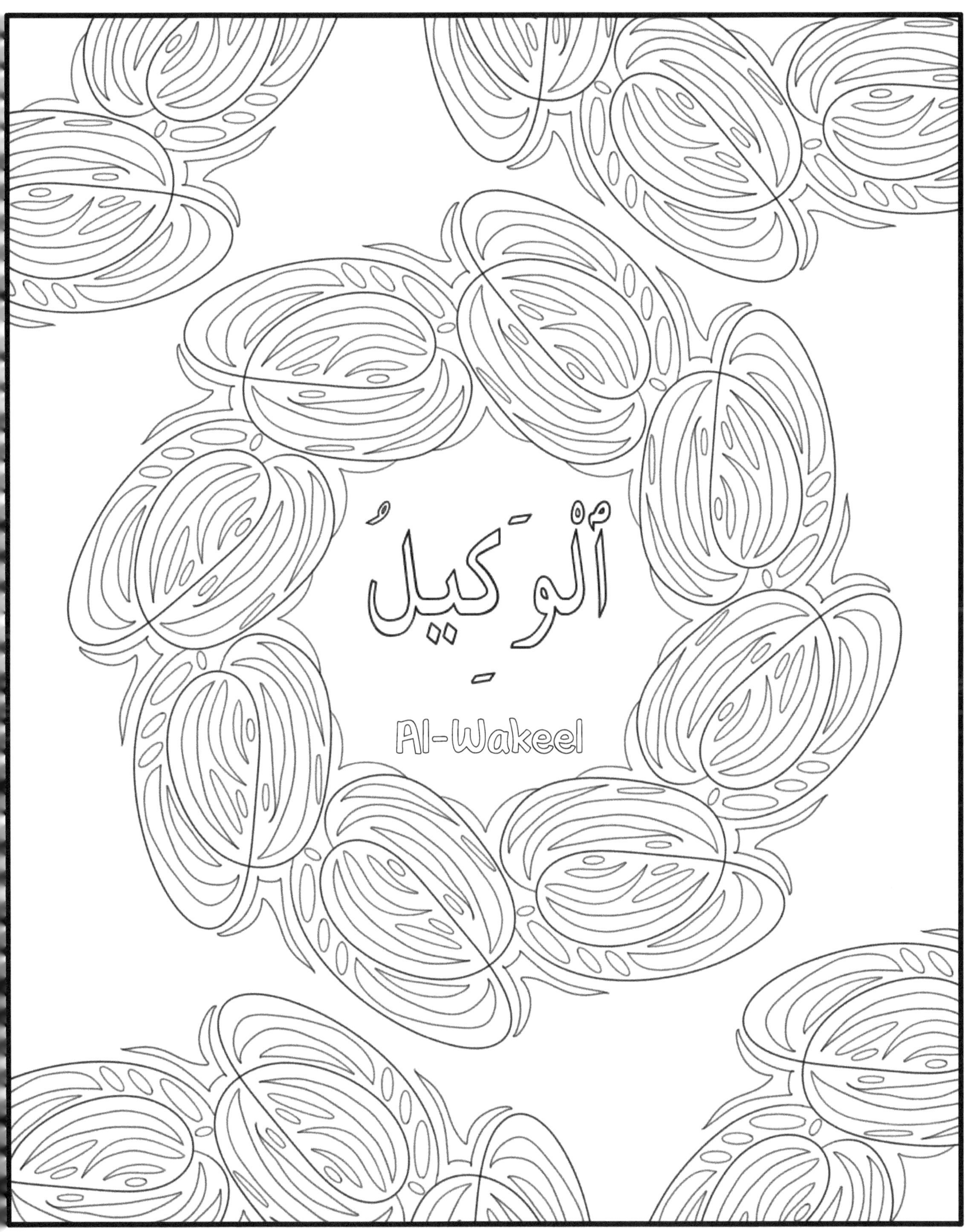

The Strong One

The Most Strong, The Strong, The One with the complete Power

The Firm One

The One with extreme Power which is un-interrupted and He does not get tired.

The Protecting Associate

The Protecting Friend, The Supporter.

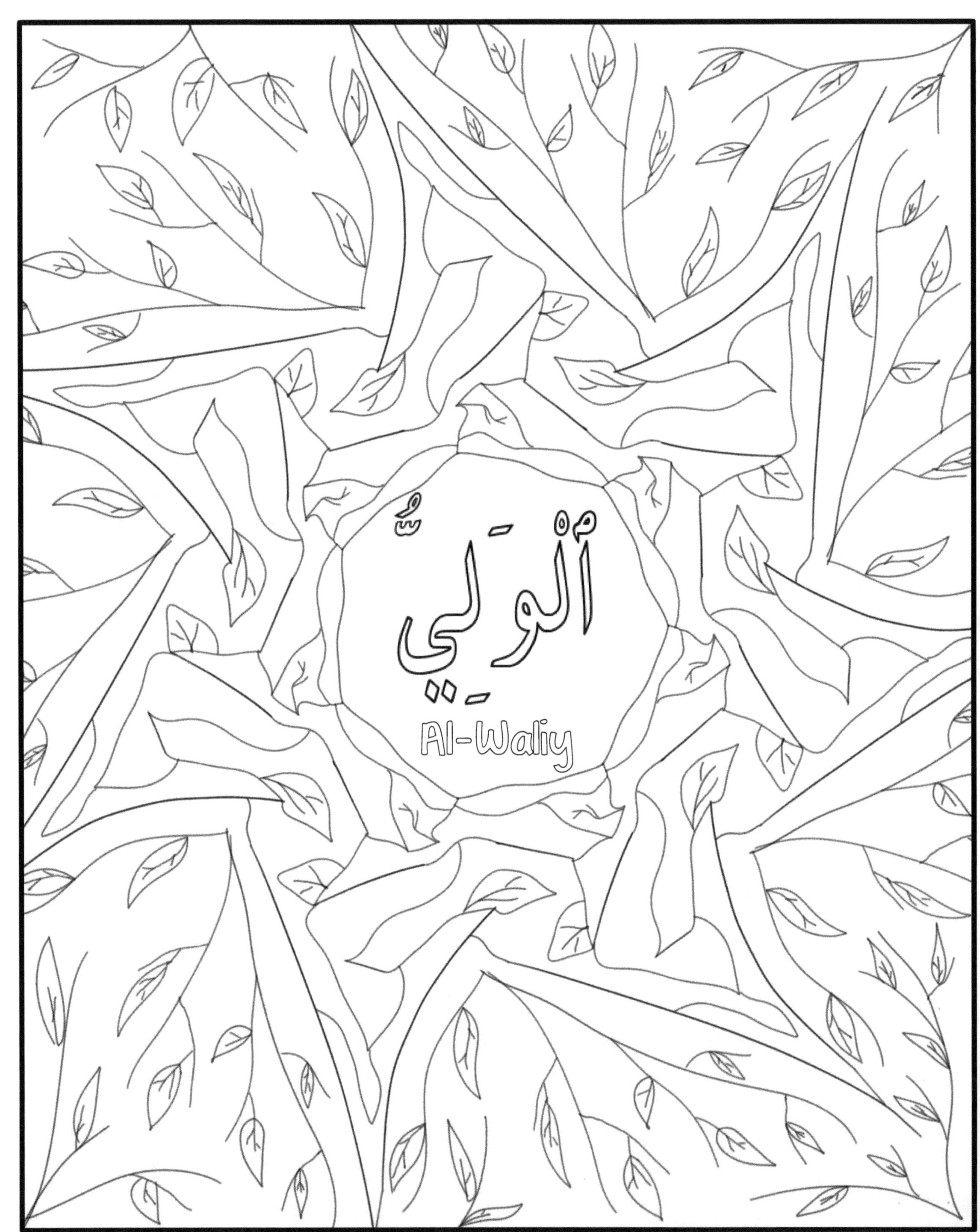

The Only Praiseworthy One

The praised One who deserves to be praised.

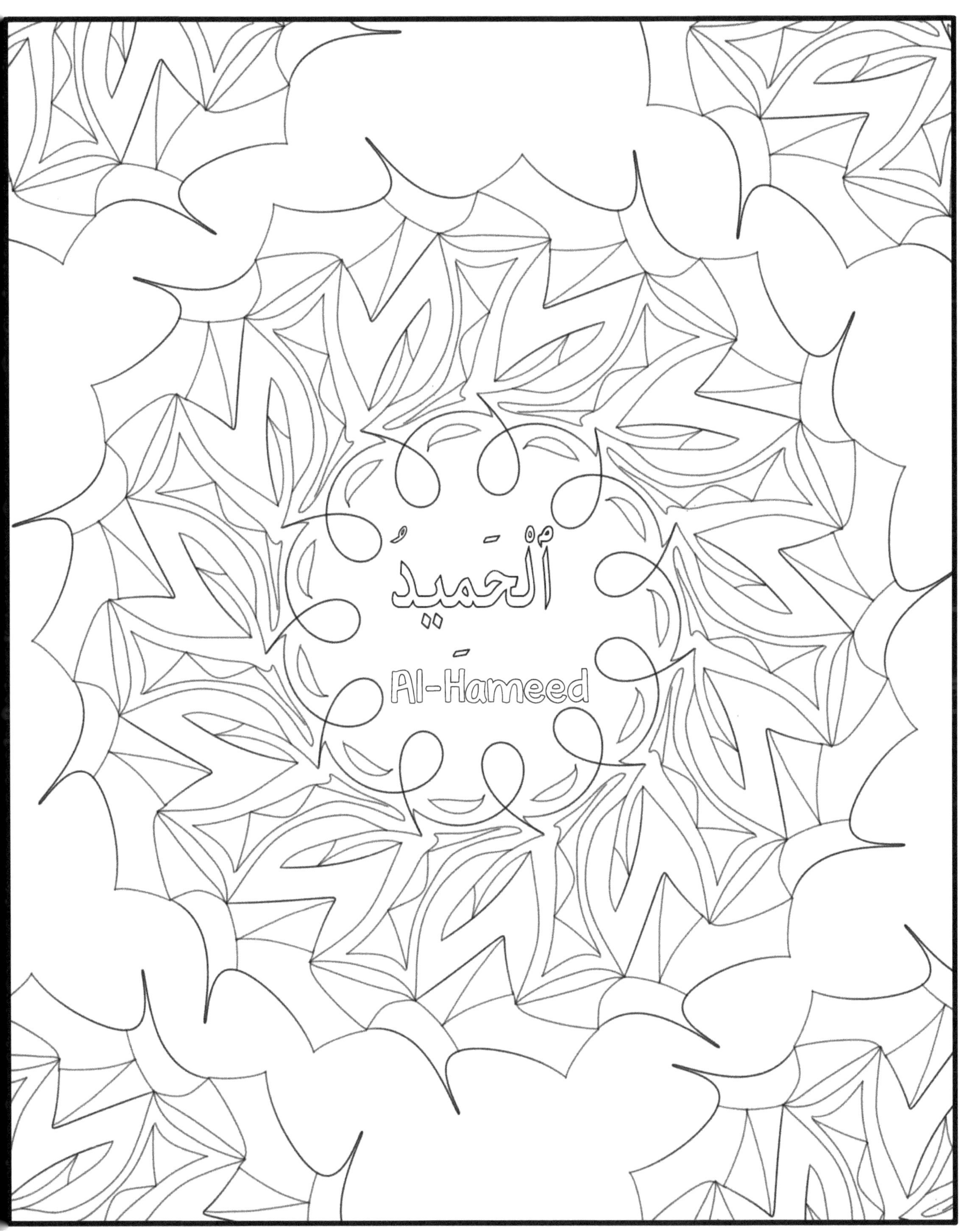

The All-Enumerating One

The Counter, The Reckoner, The One who the count of things are known to him.

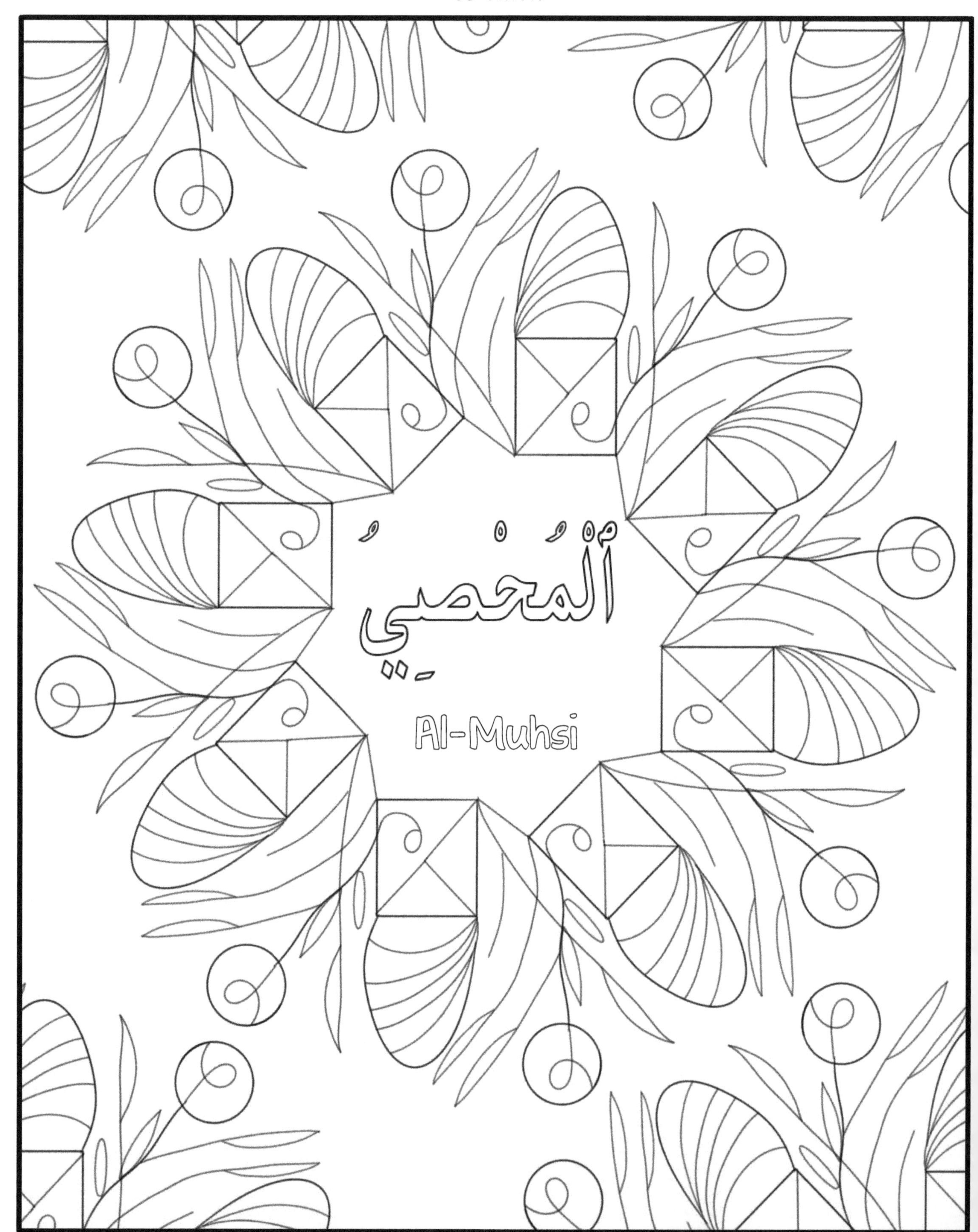

The Originator

The One who started the human being. That is, He created him.

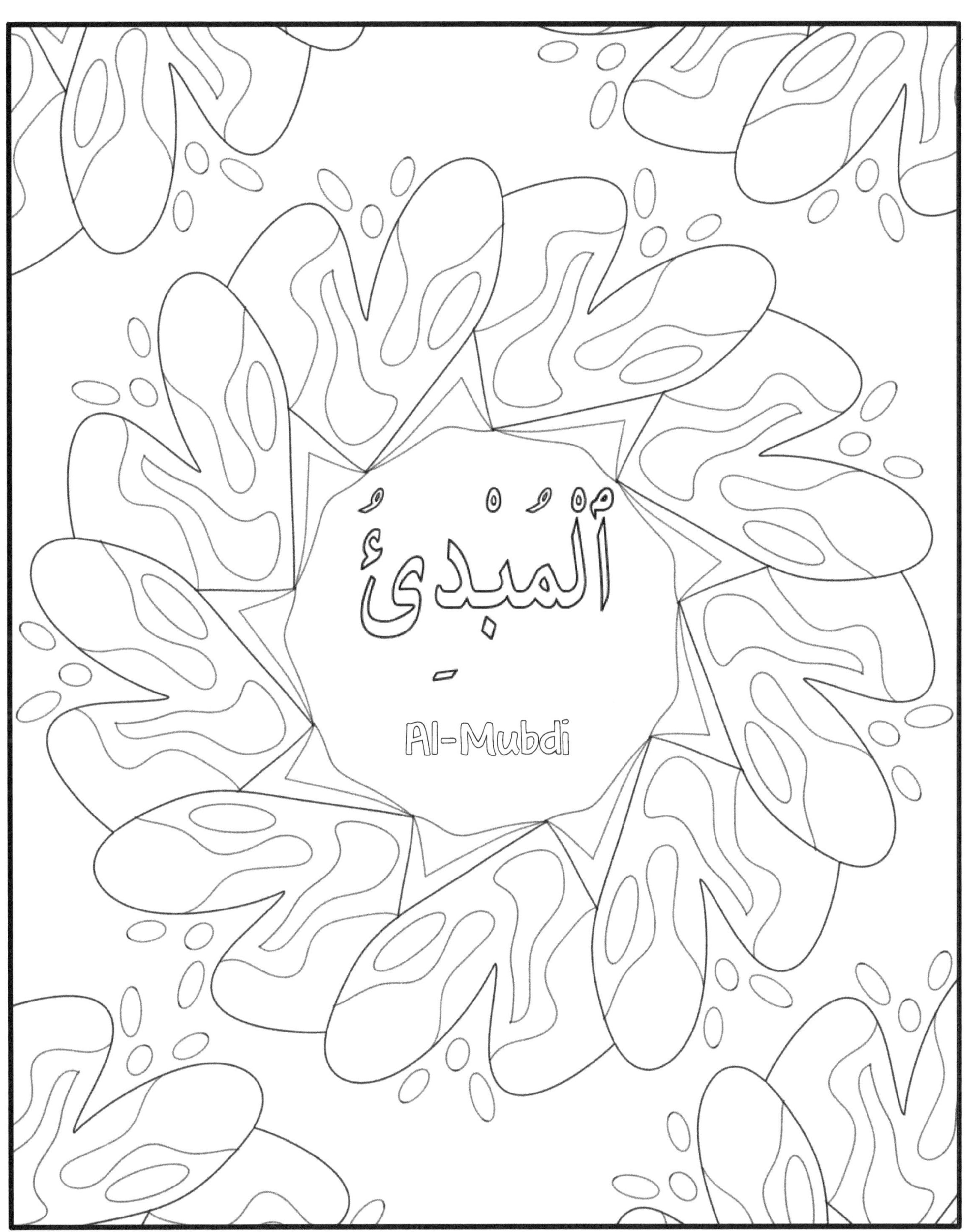

The Restorer

The Reproducer, The One who brings back the creatures after death

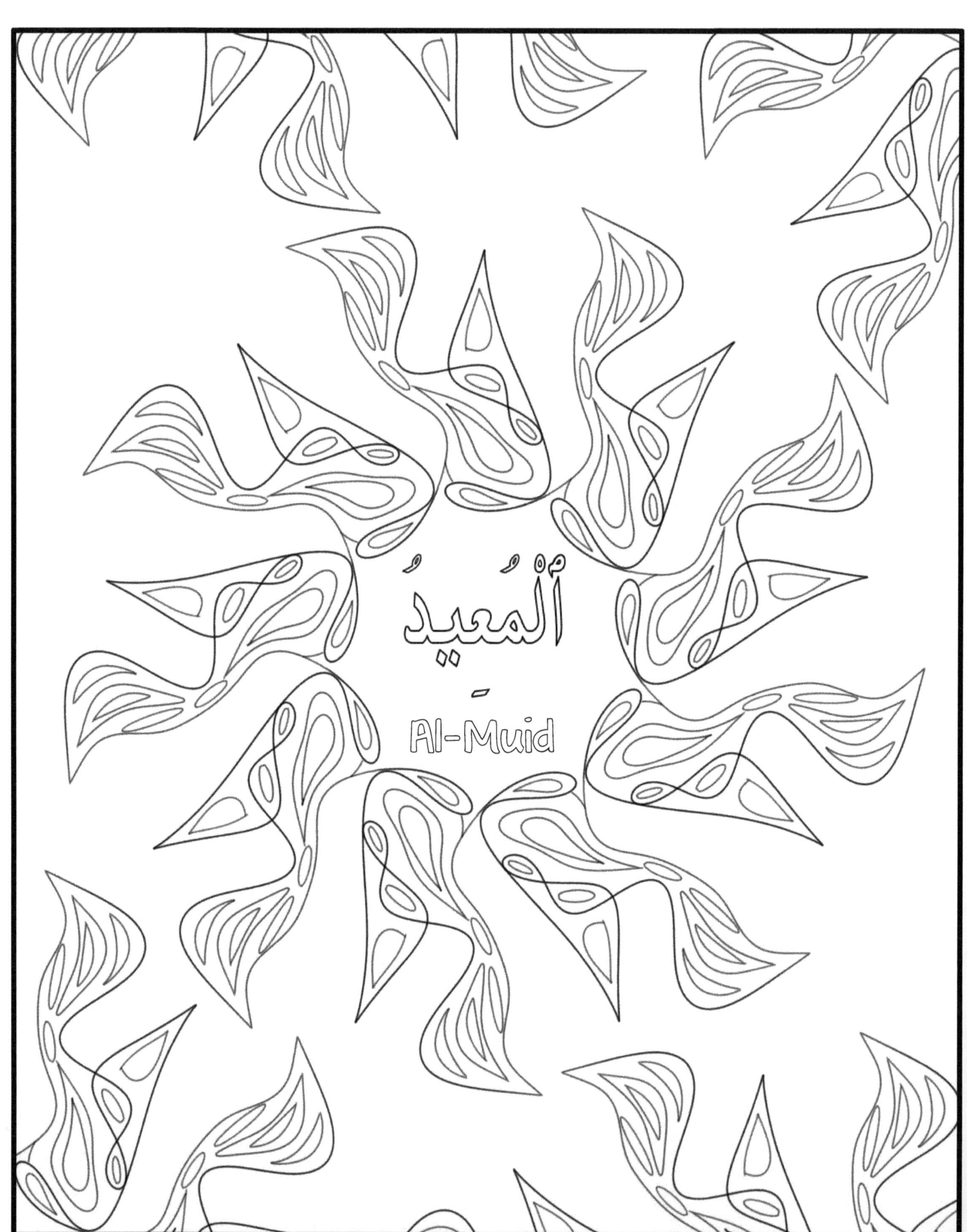

The Maintainer of Life

The Restorer, The Giver of Life.

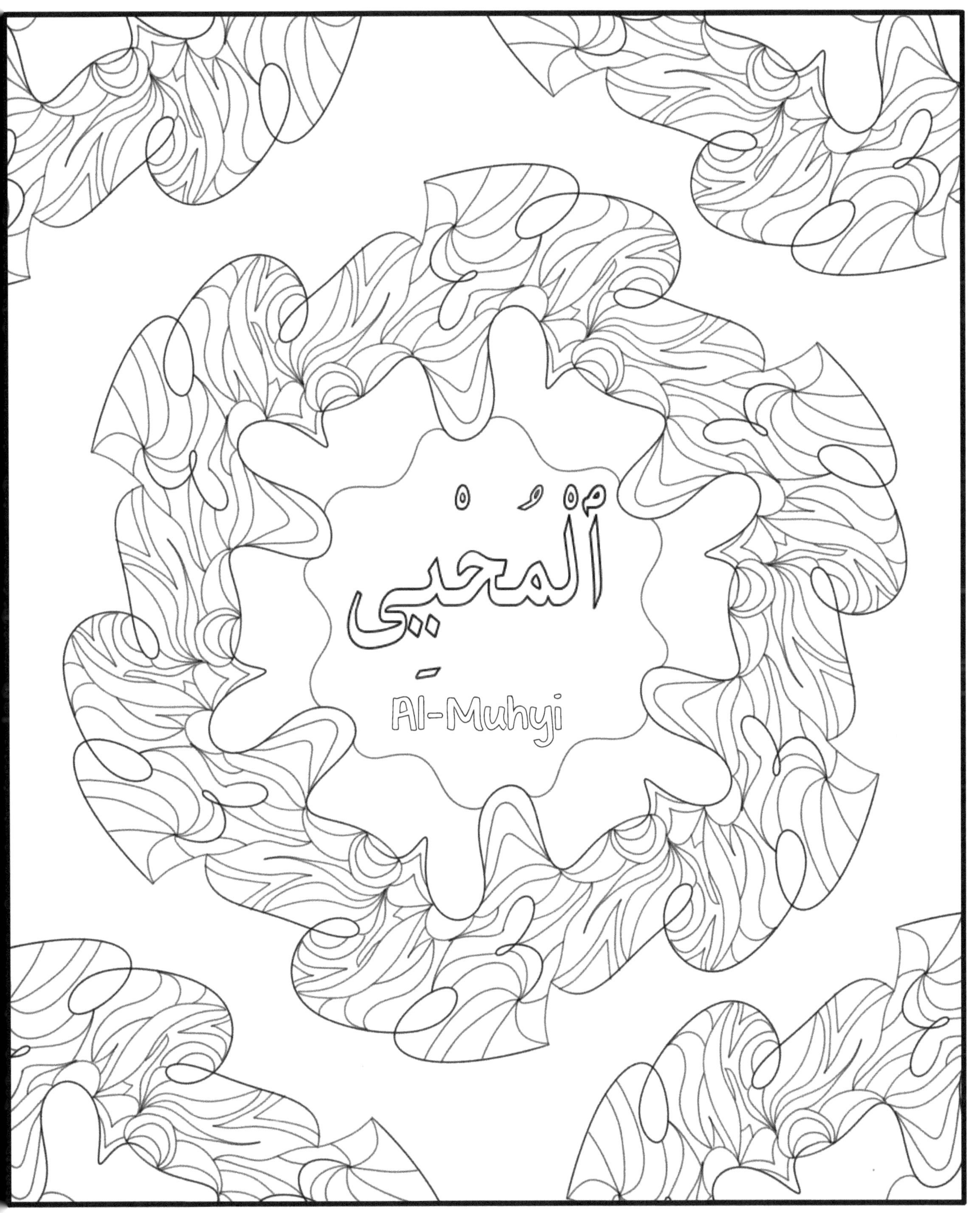

The Inflictor of Death

The Creator of Death, The Destroyer, The One who renders the living dead.

The Eternally Living One

The Alive, The One attributed with a life that is unlike our life and is not that of a combination of soul, flesh or blood.

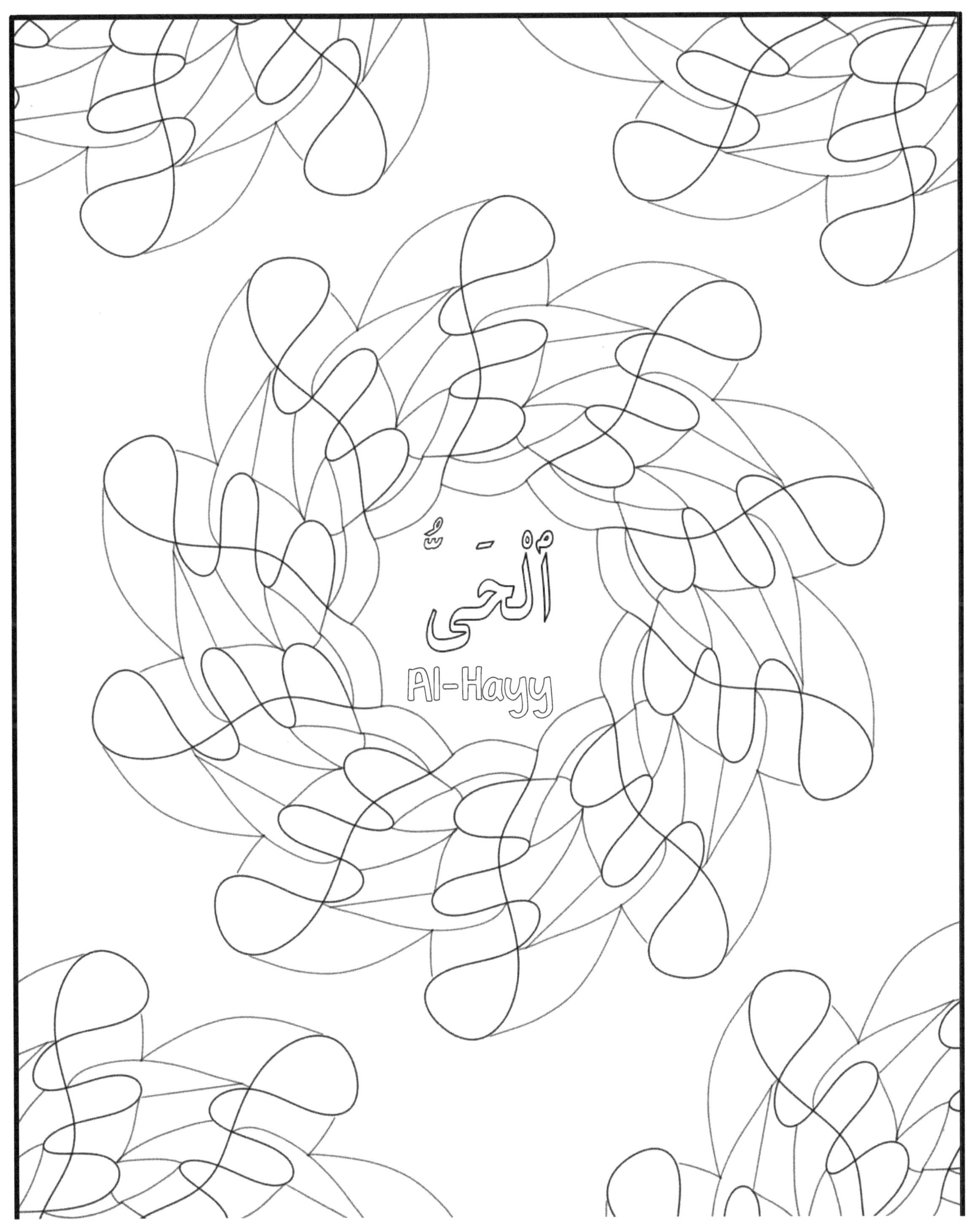

The Self Subsisting One

The Self-Subsisting, The Self-Existing One upon Whom all others depend

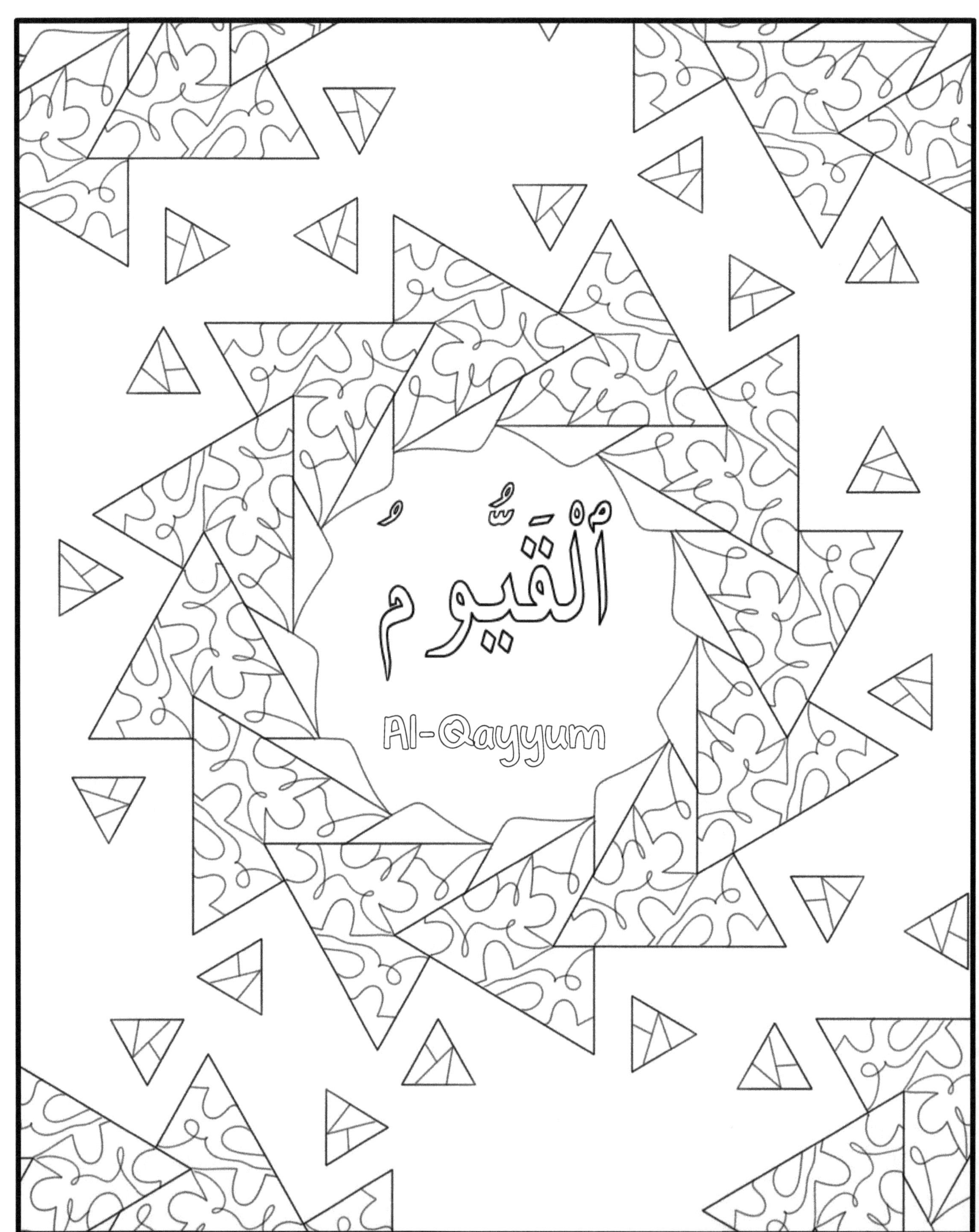

The Perceiver

The Finder, The Rich who is never poor. Al-Wajid is Richness.

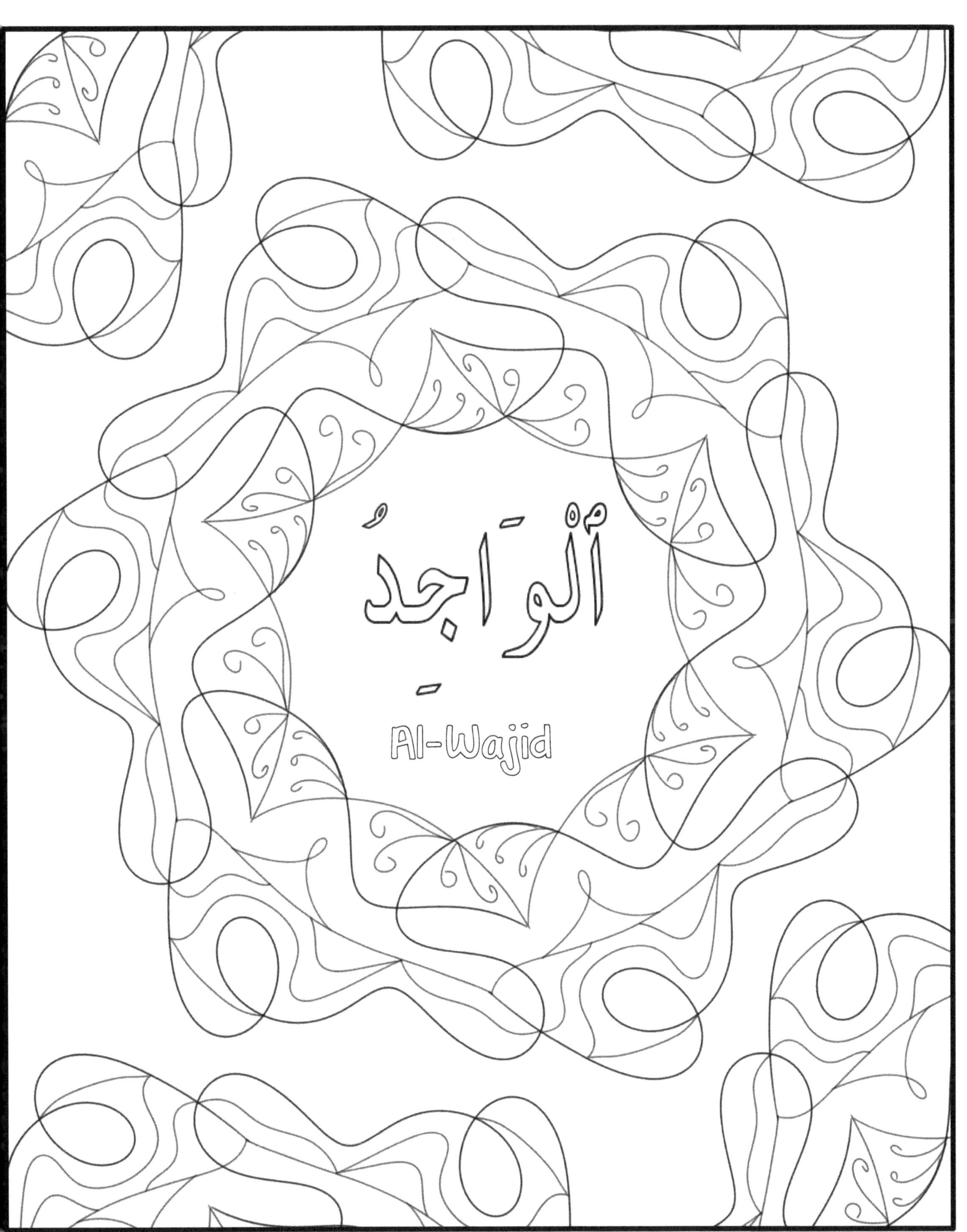

The Noble One

The Glorious, He who is Most Glorious..

The Only One

The Unique, The One, The One without a partner..

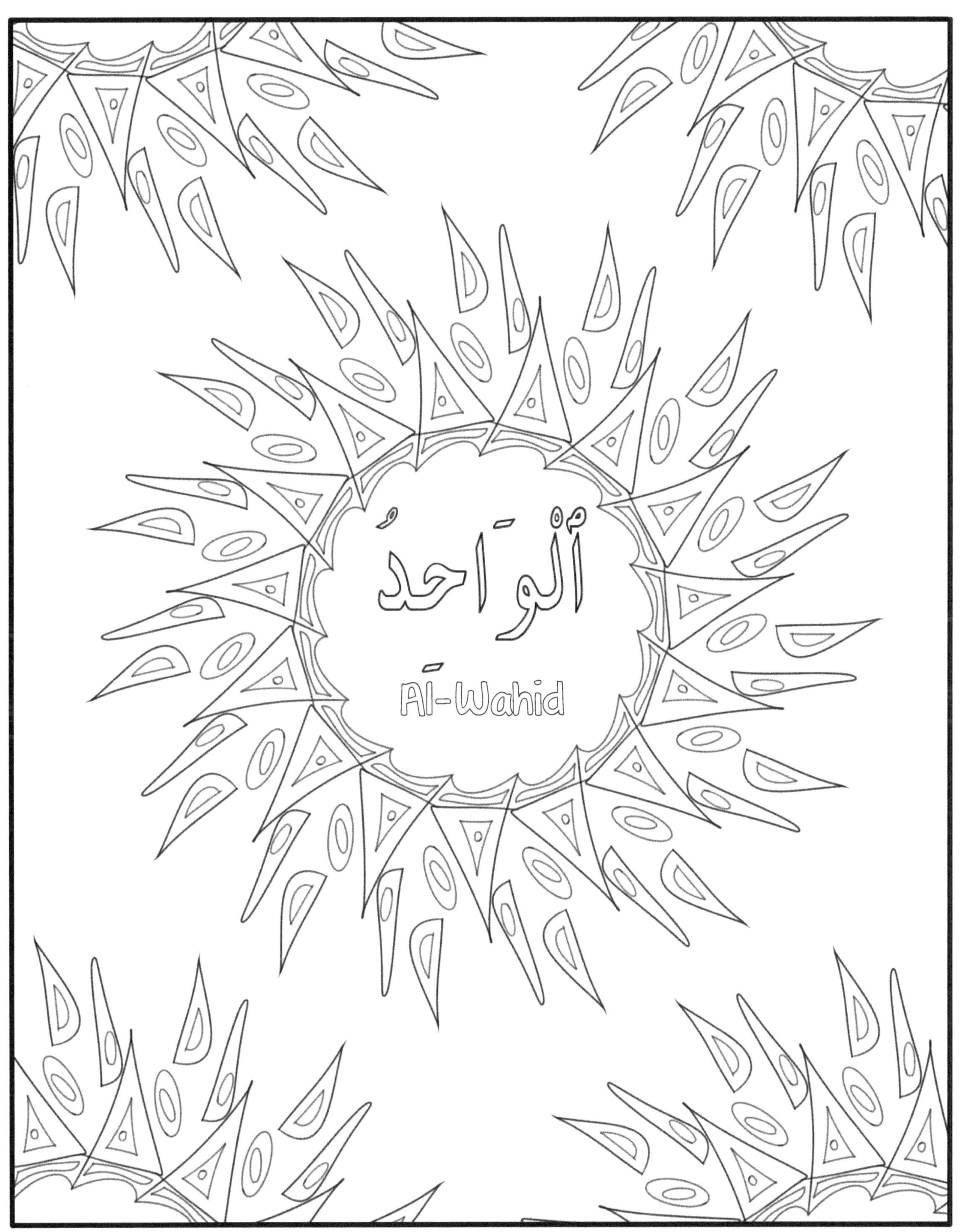

Al-Ahad describes absolute oneness and uniqueness; none compares to Him. In contrast to Al-Wahid which refers to the numerical one.

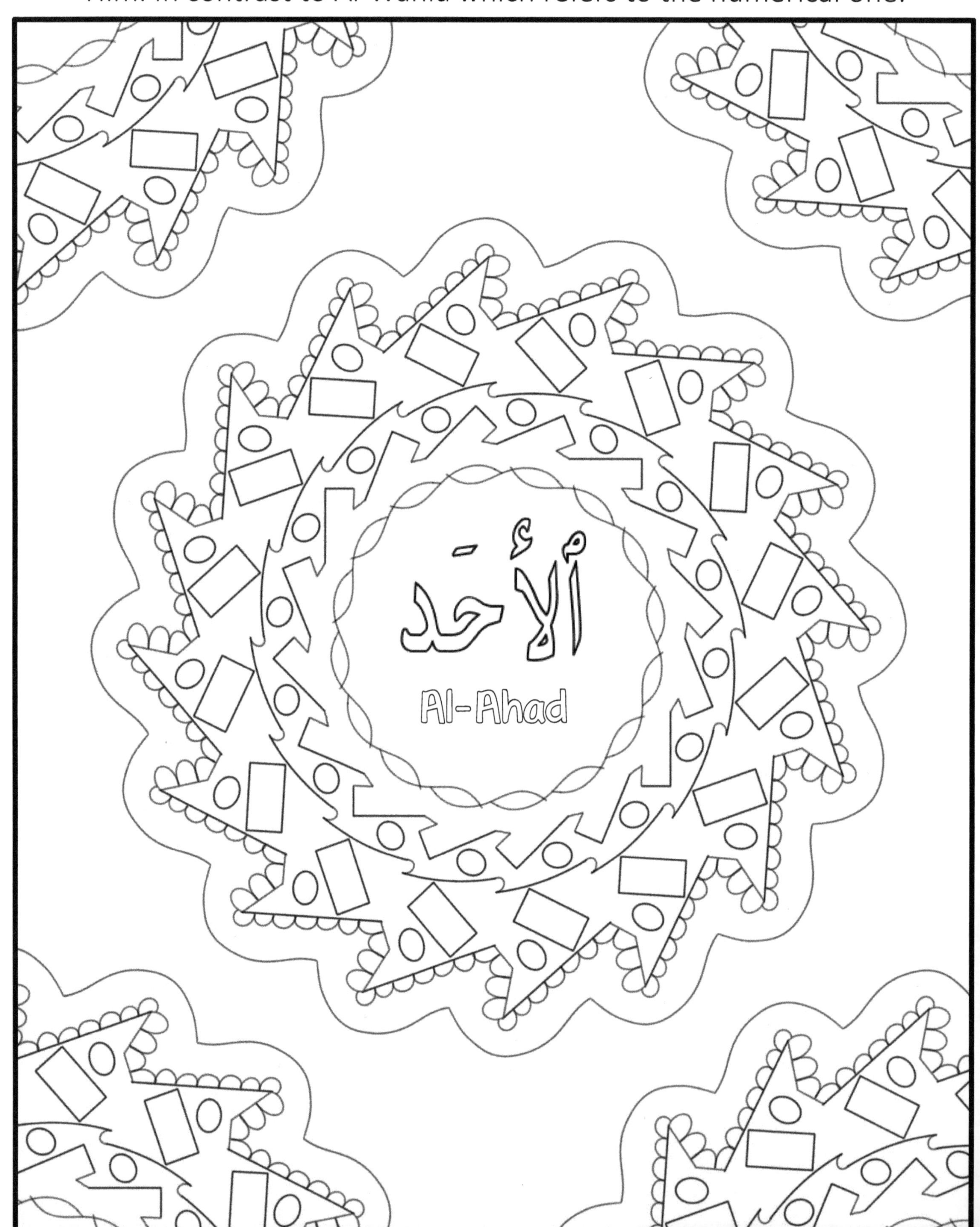

The Supreme Provider

The Master who is relied upon in matters and reverted to in ones needs.
He is the only one a person should turn to when feeling helpless.

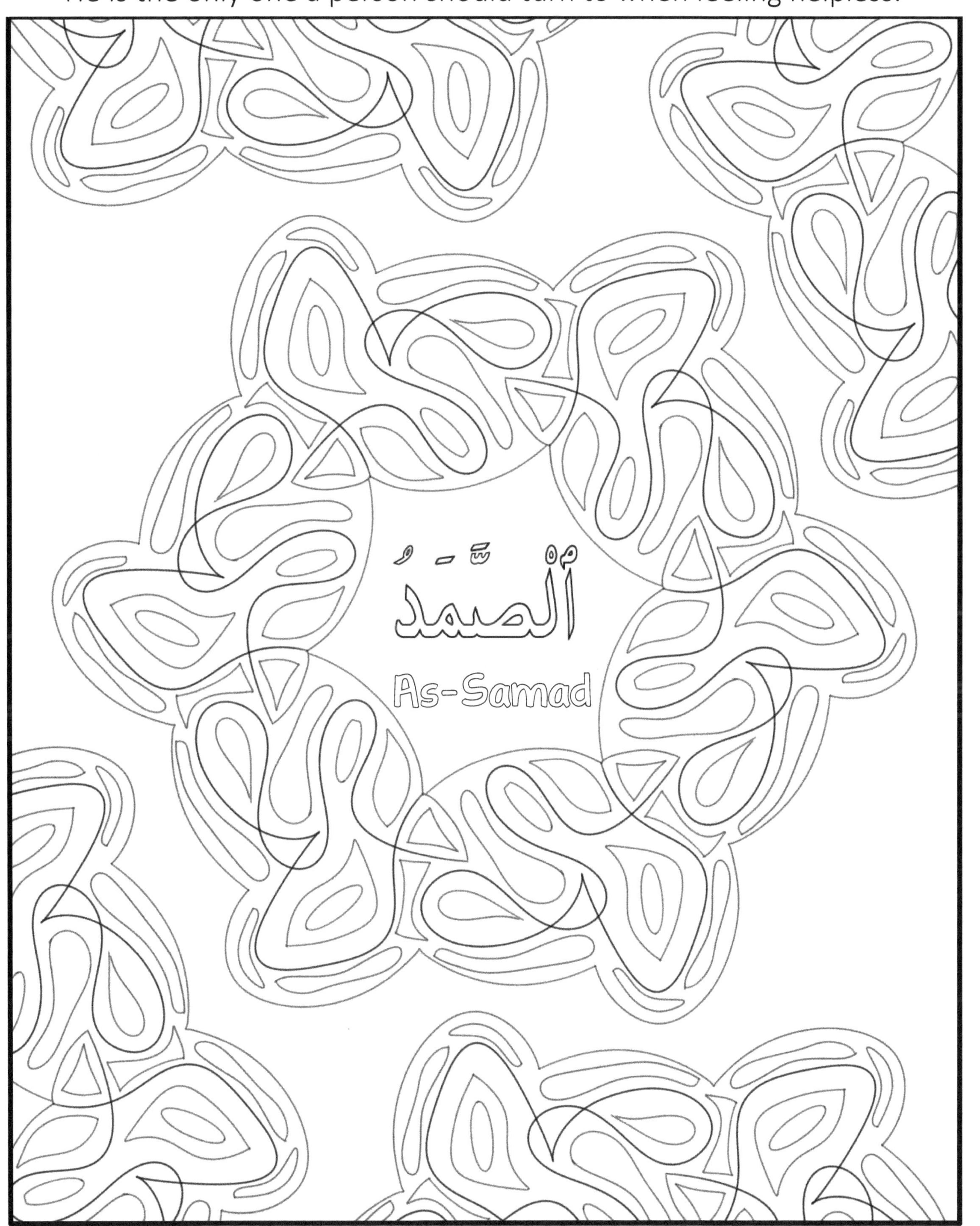

The All Powerful

The Able, The Capable, The One attributed with Power.

The All-Authoritative One

The Powerful, The Dominant, The One with the perfect Power that nothing is withheld from Him.

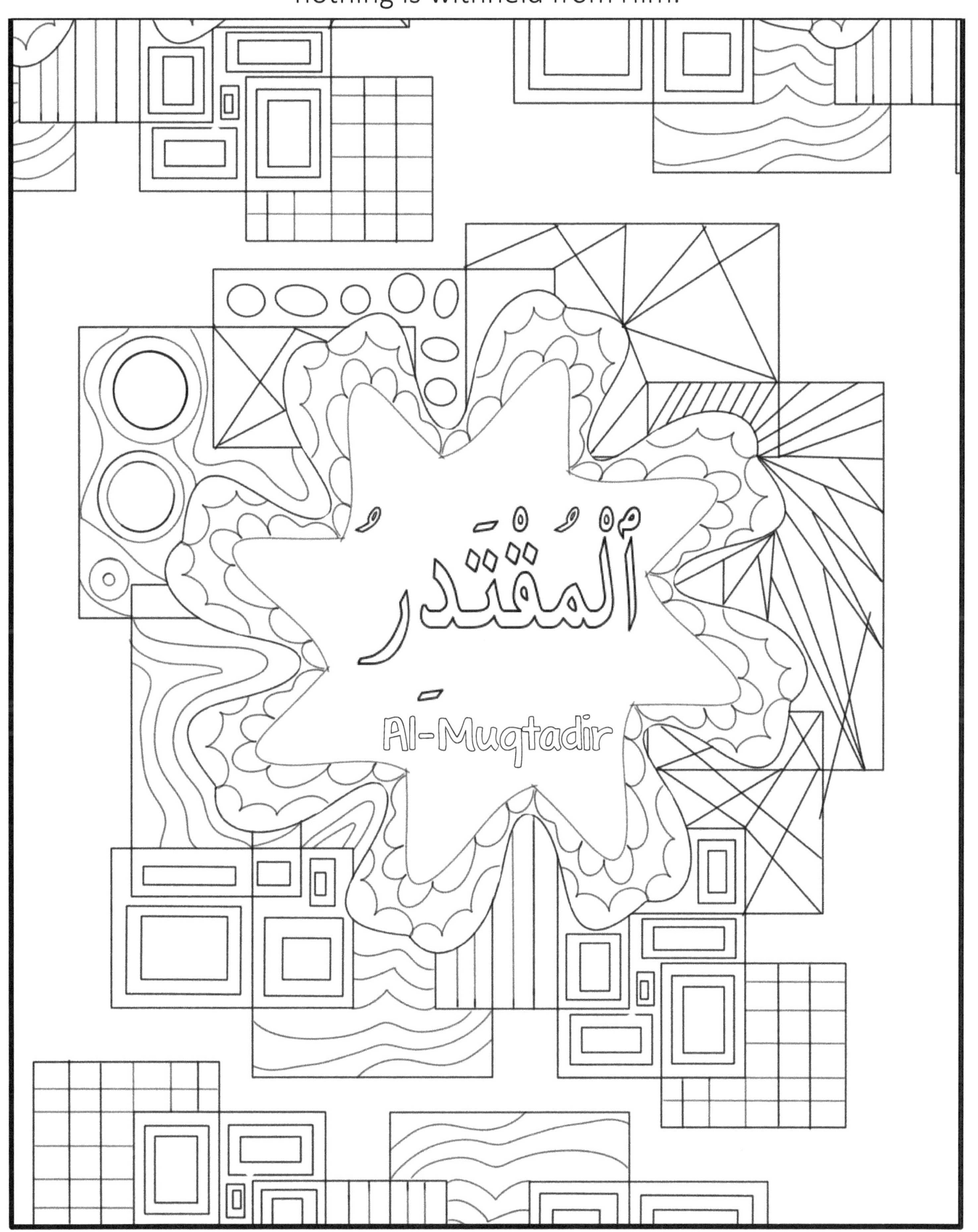

The Expediting One

The Expediter, The Promoter, The One who puts things in their right places.

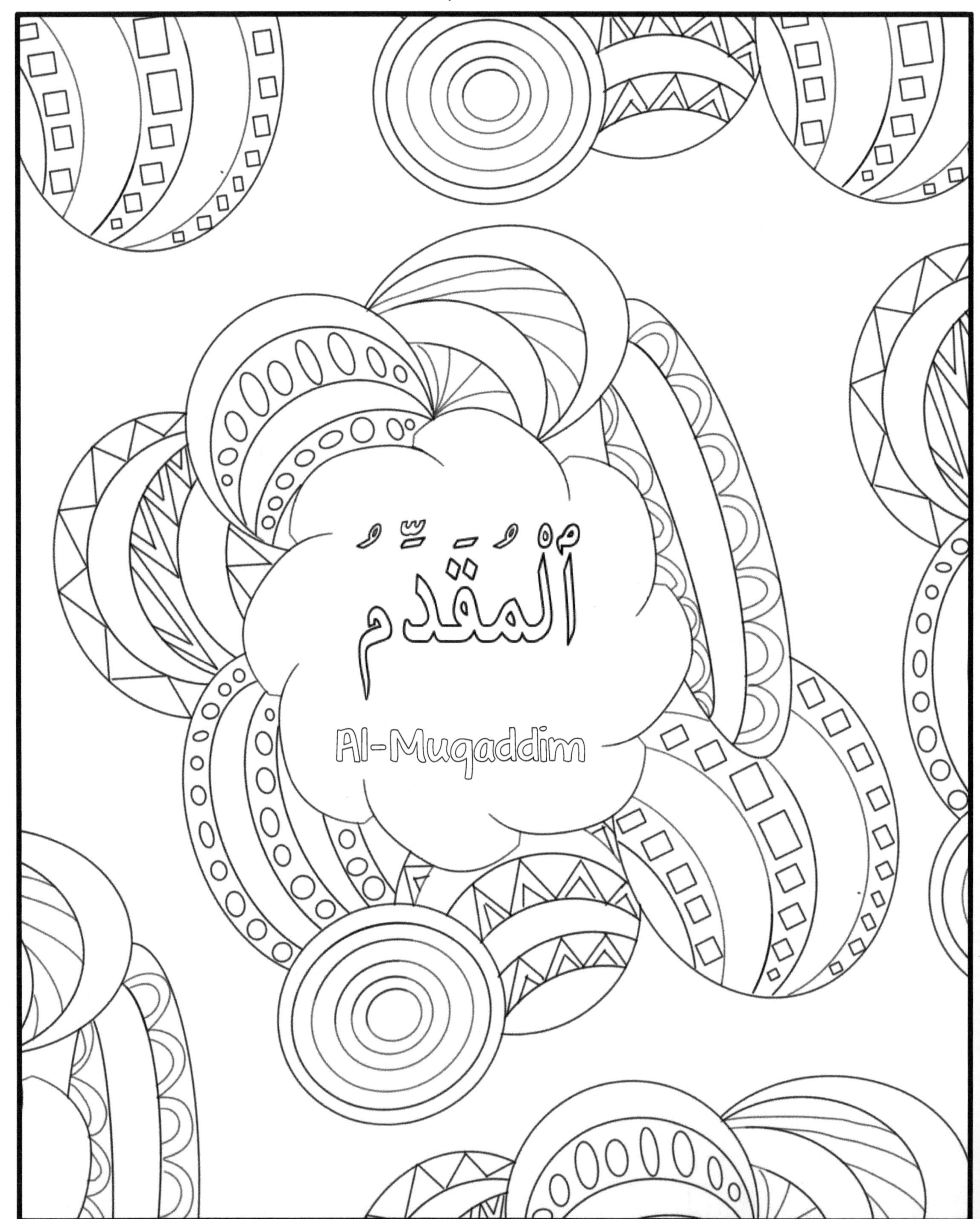

The Delayer

The Postponer, He makes ahead what He wills and delays what He wills.

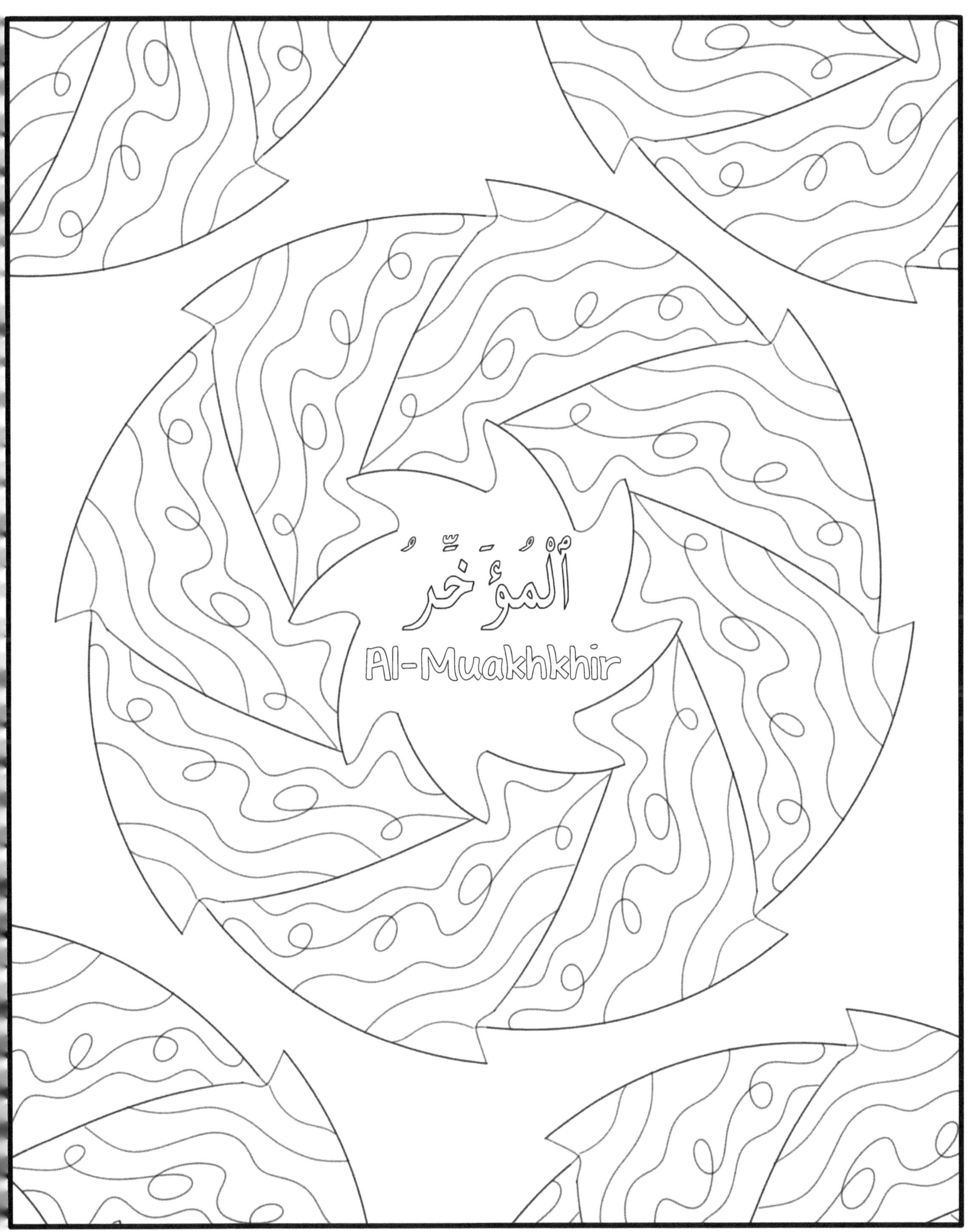

The Very First

The First, The One whose Existence is without a beginning.

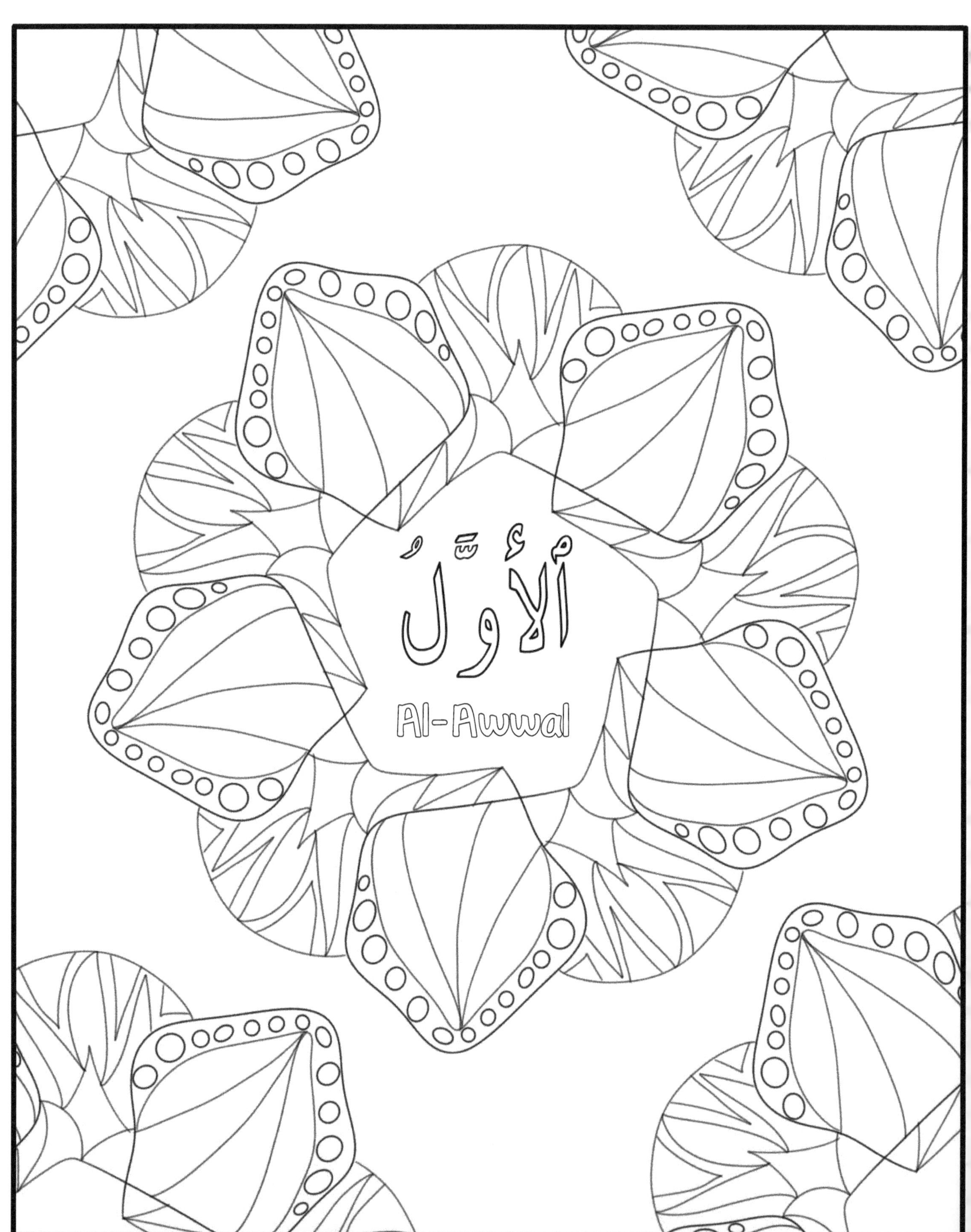

The Infinite Last One

The Last, The One whose Existence is without an end.

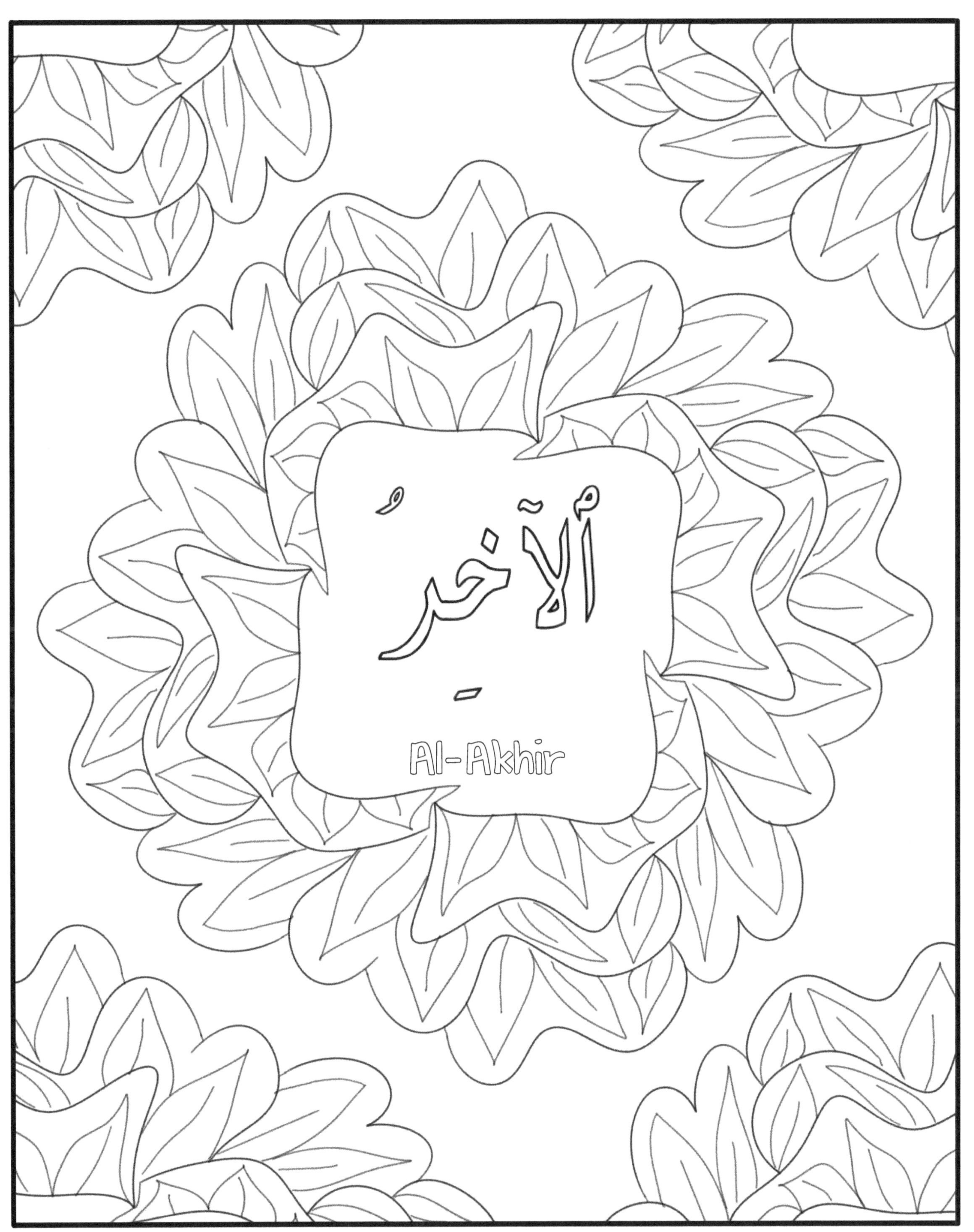

The Perceptible

The Manifest, The Conspicuous, The Evident.

The Imperceptible

The Hidden, The Secret One, The Inner One, The Knower of Hidden Things

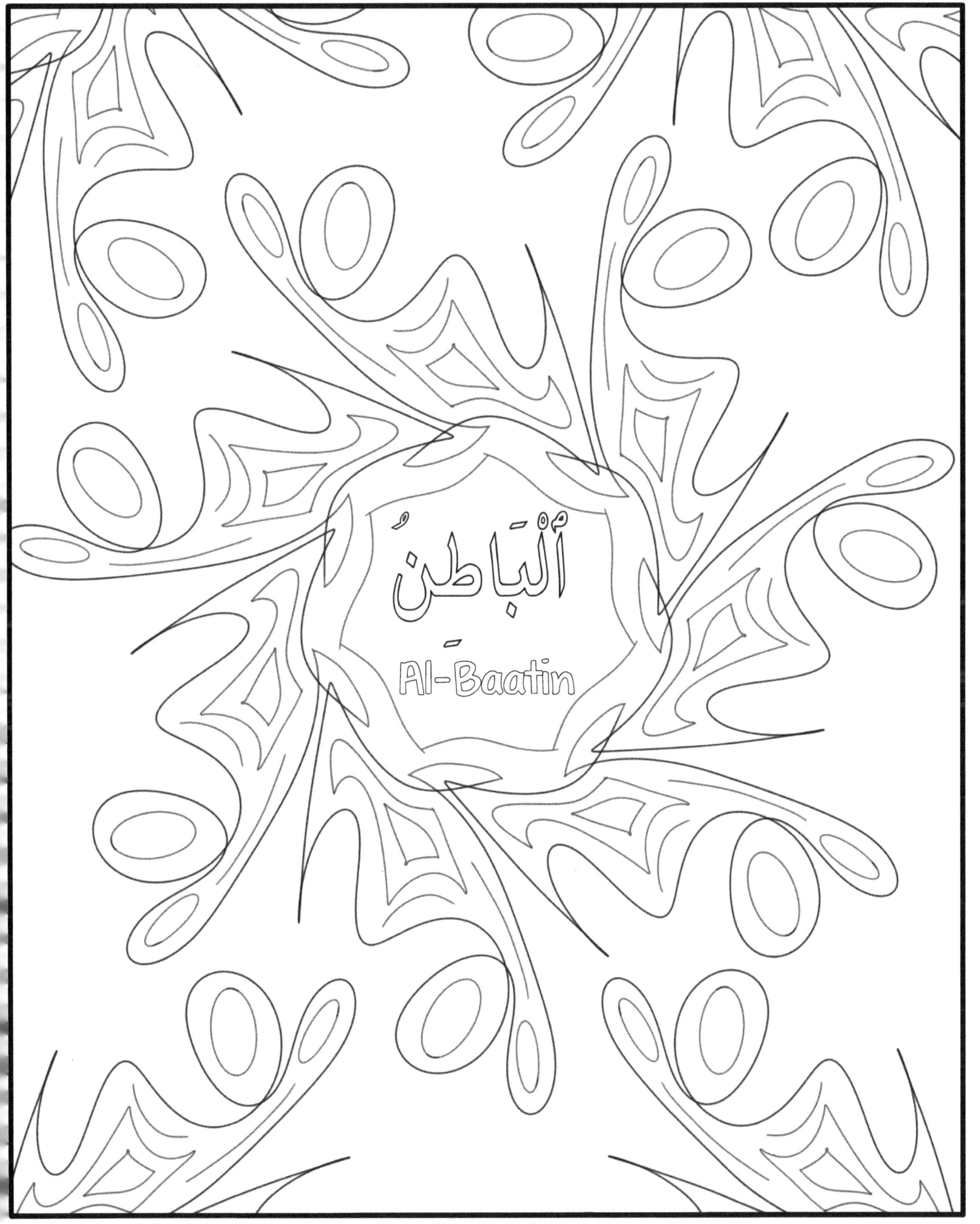

The Governor, The One who owns things and manages them.

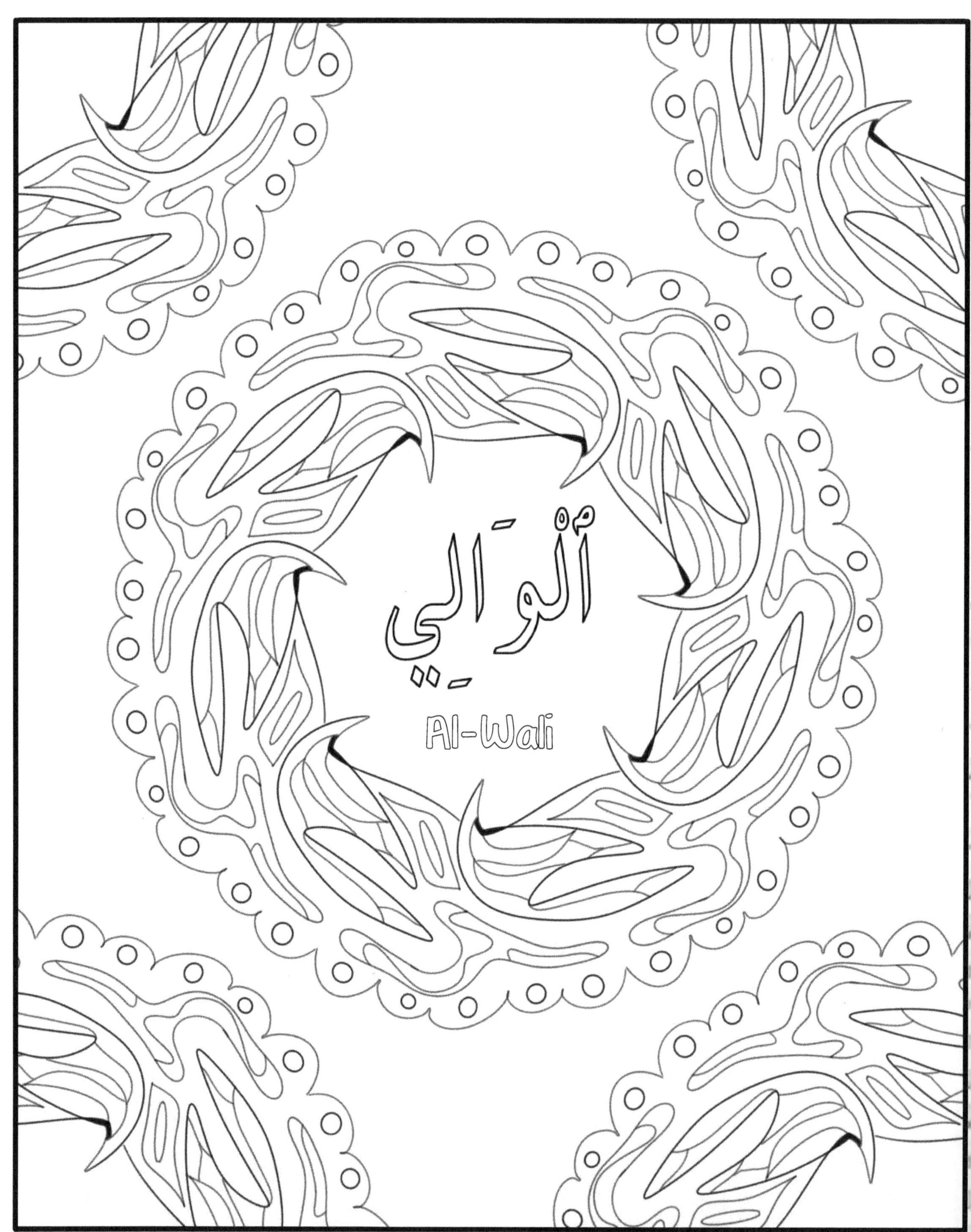

The Extremely Exalted One

The Most Exalted, The High Exalted, The One who is clear from the attributes of the creation.

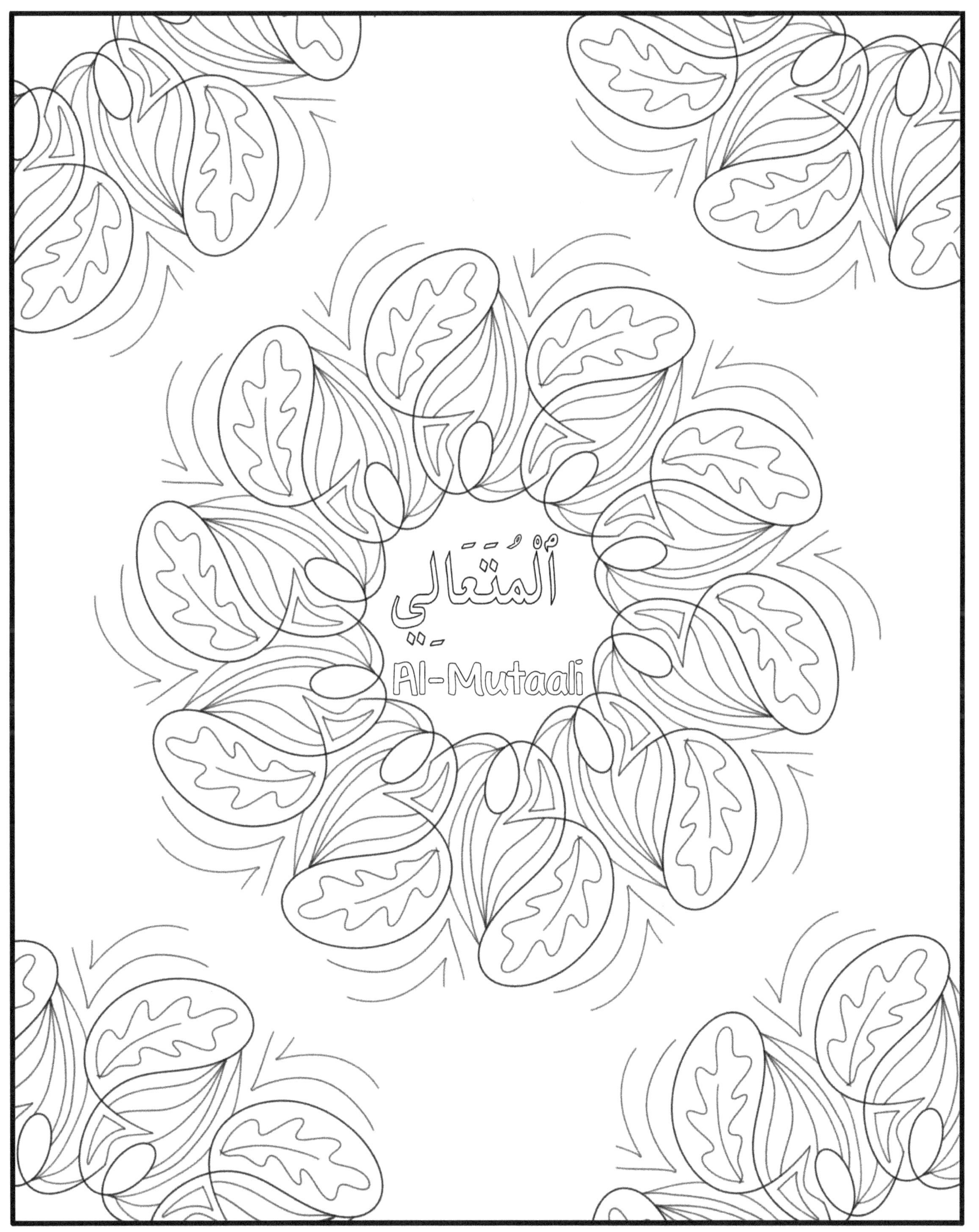

The Source of All Goodness

The Righteous, The One who is kind to His creatures

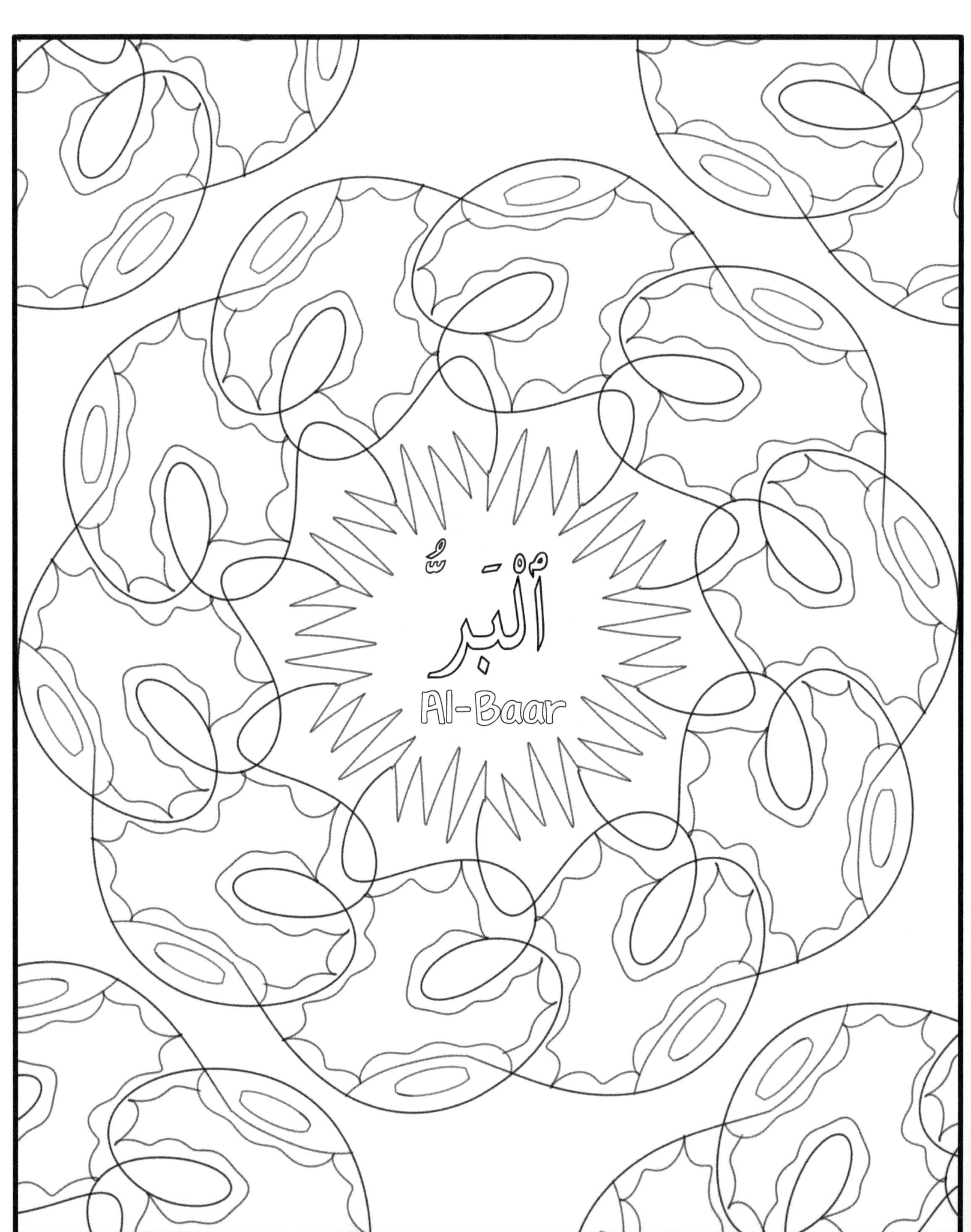

The Acceptor of Repentance

The Oft-Forgiving, The Acceptor of our Return

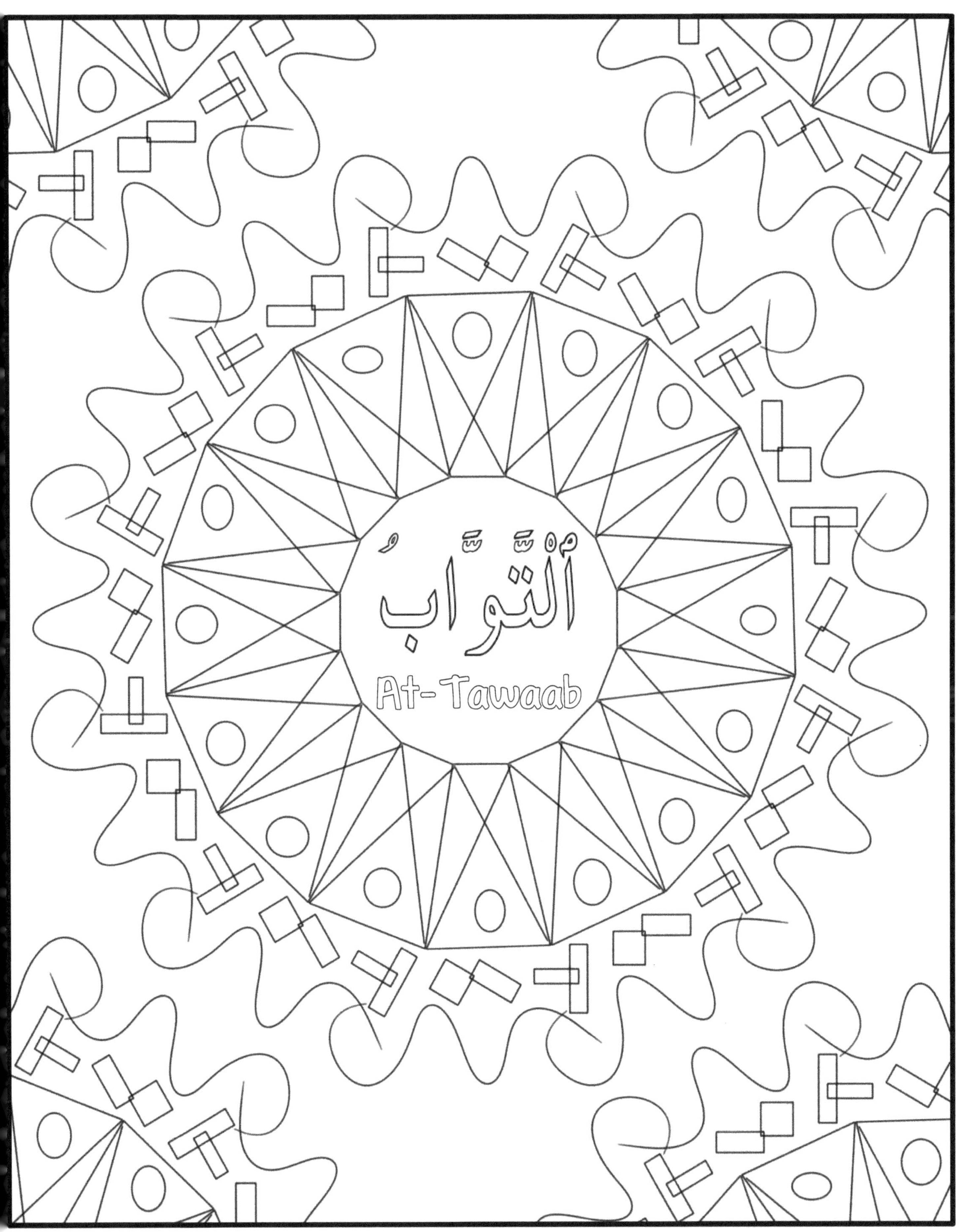

The Retaliator

The Avenger, The Disapprover, The Inflictor of Retribution

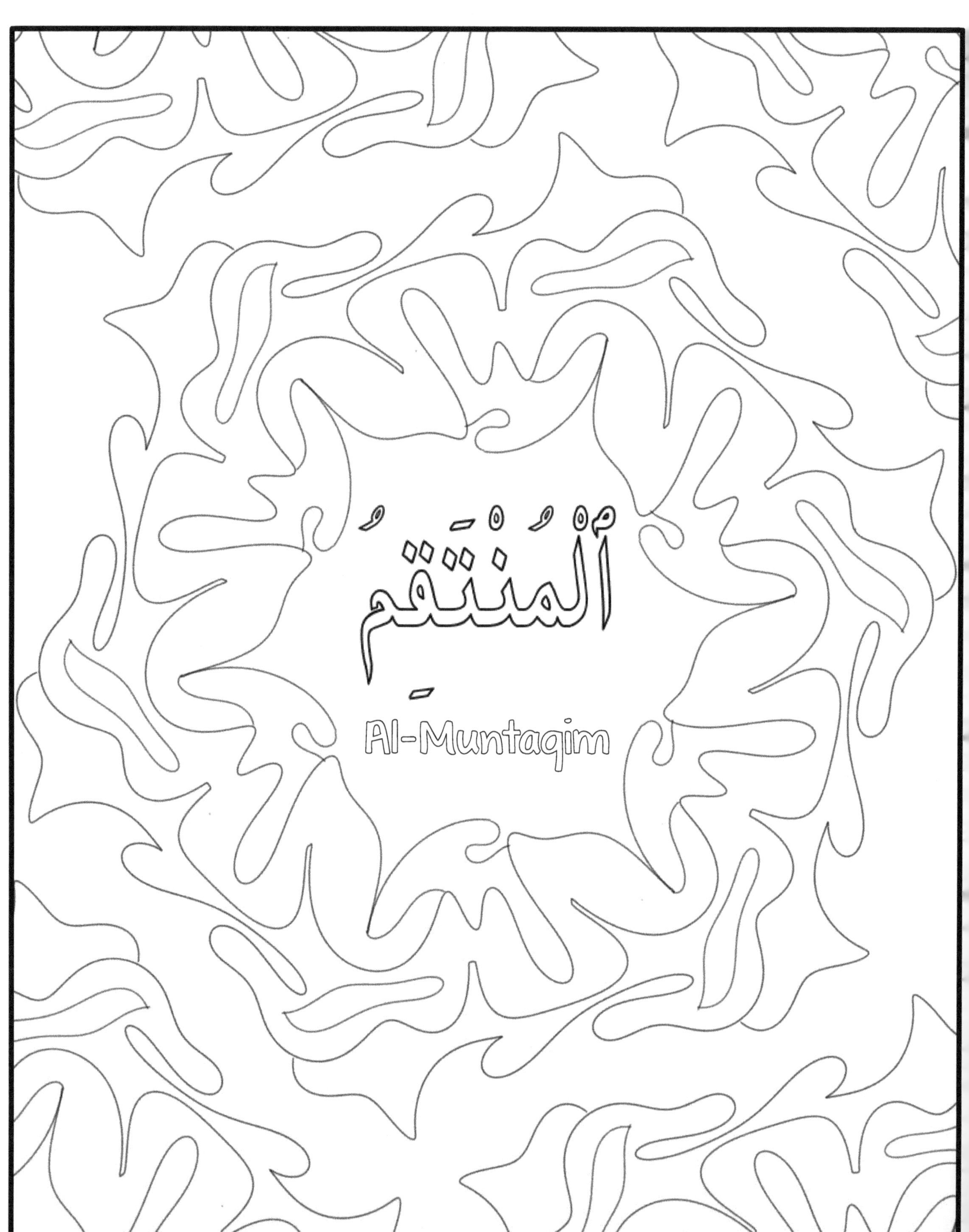

The Supreme Pardoner

The Pardoner, The Forgiver and The Eliminator of Sins.

The Benign One

The Most Kind, The Tenderly Merciful, The Clement and Compassionate.

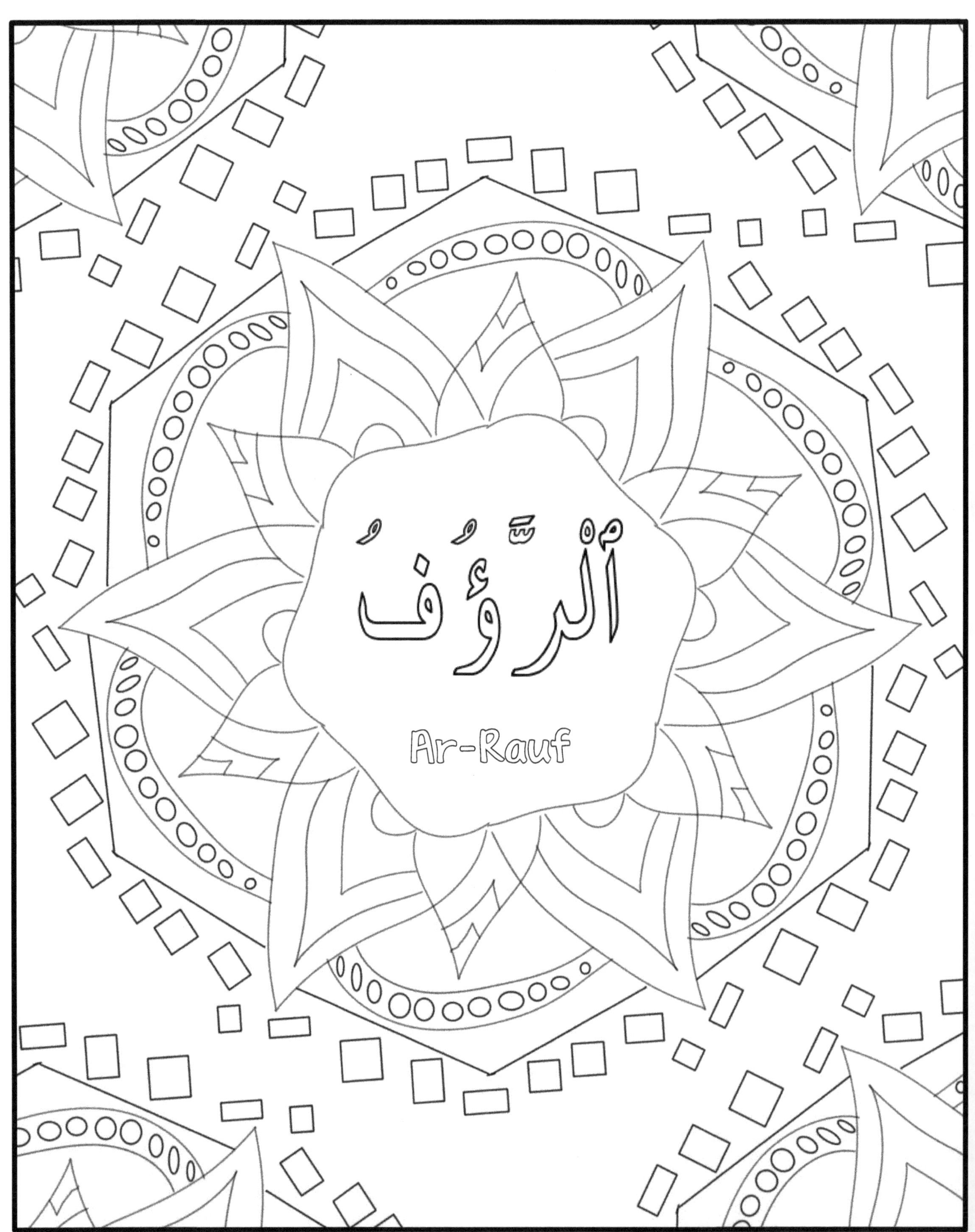

The Eternal Possessor of Sovereignty

The One who controls the Dominion and gives dominion to whoever He wills.

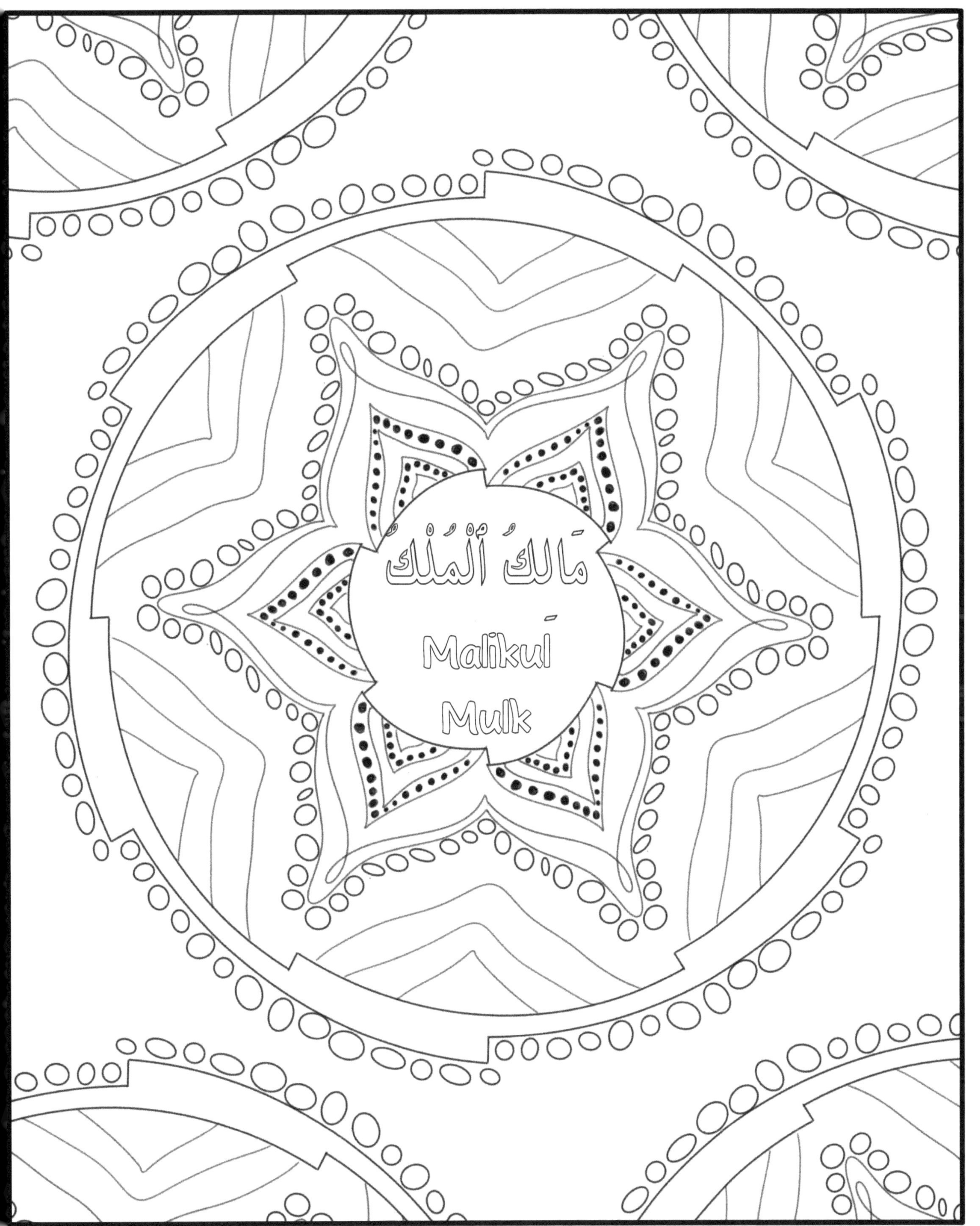

The Lord of Majesty and Bounty.

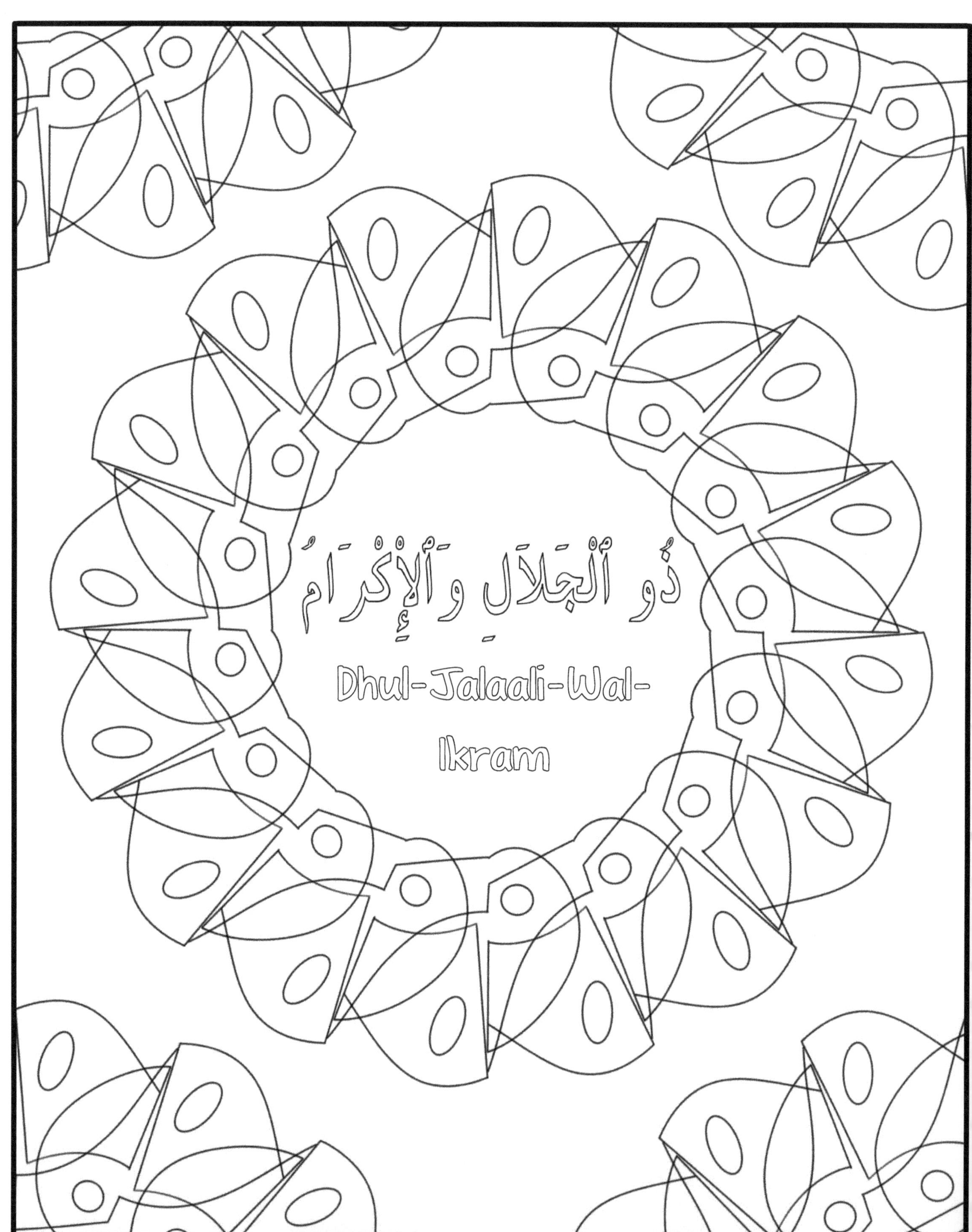

The Just One

The Equitable, The One who is Just in His judgment.

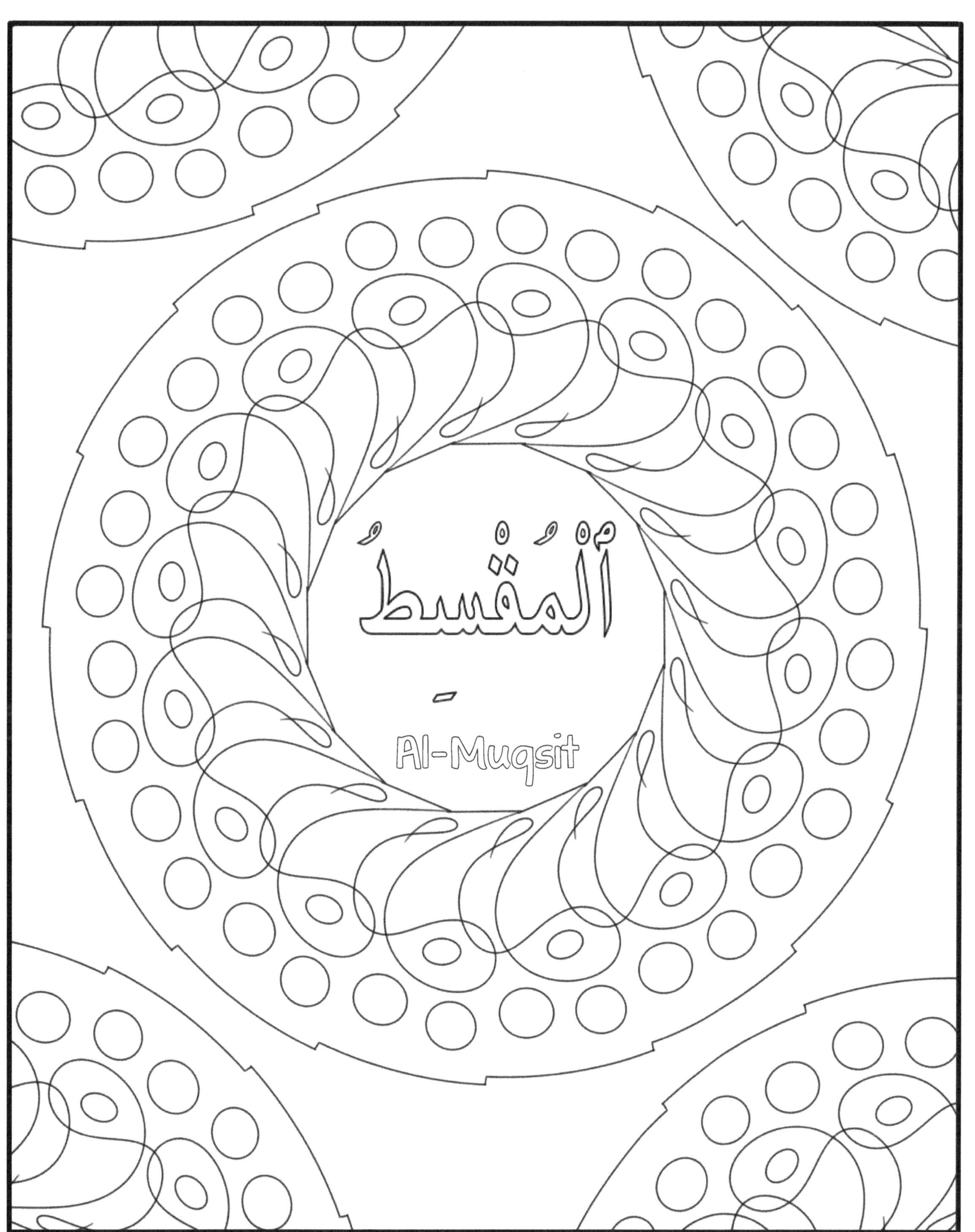

The Assembler of Scattered Creations

The Gatherer, The One who gathers the creatures on the Day of Judgment.

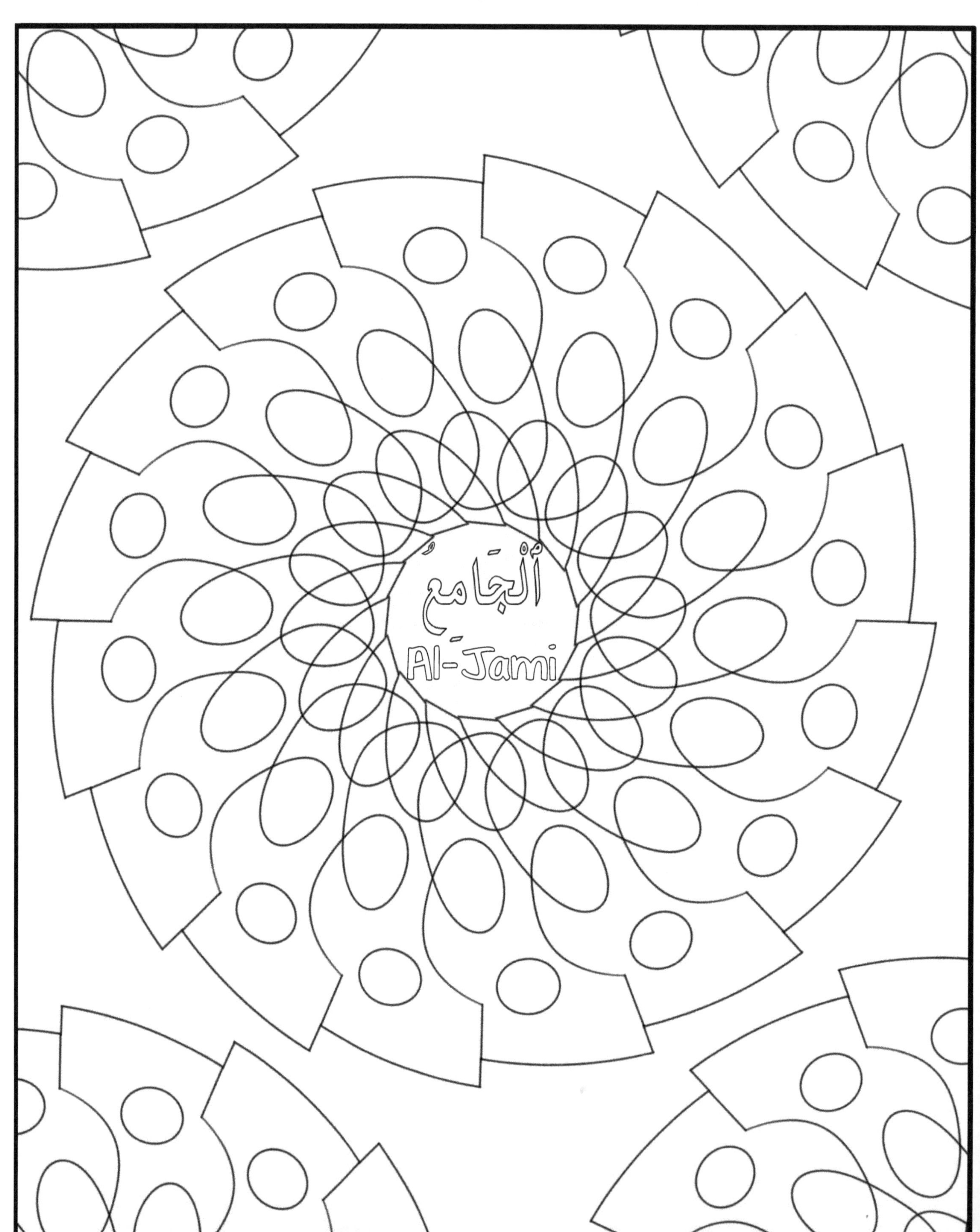

The Self Sufficient One

The One who does not need the creation.

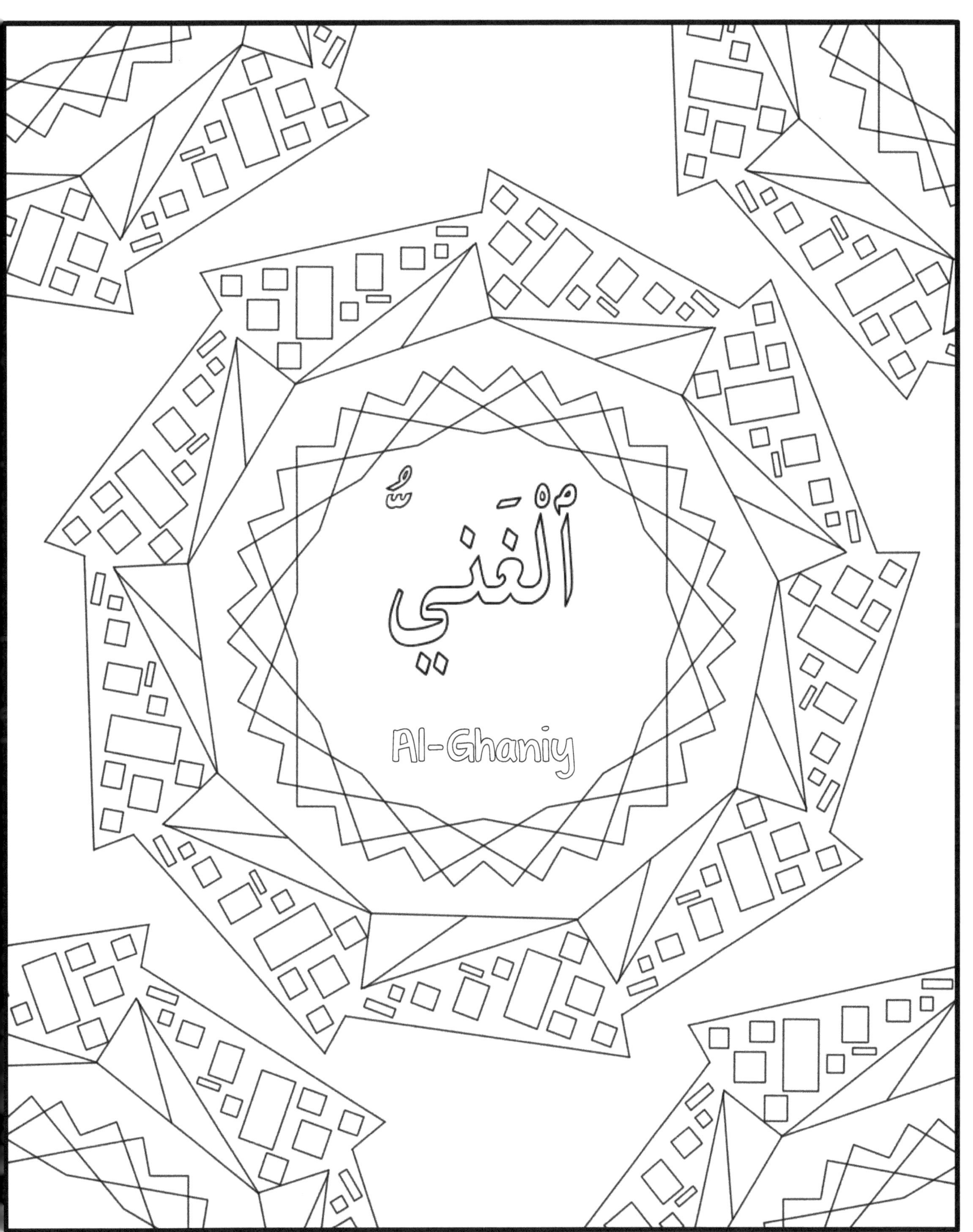

The Enricher

The Emancipator, The Fulfiller of Needs, The Bestower of Wealth.

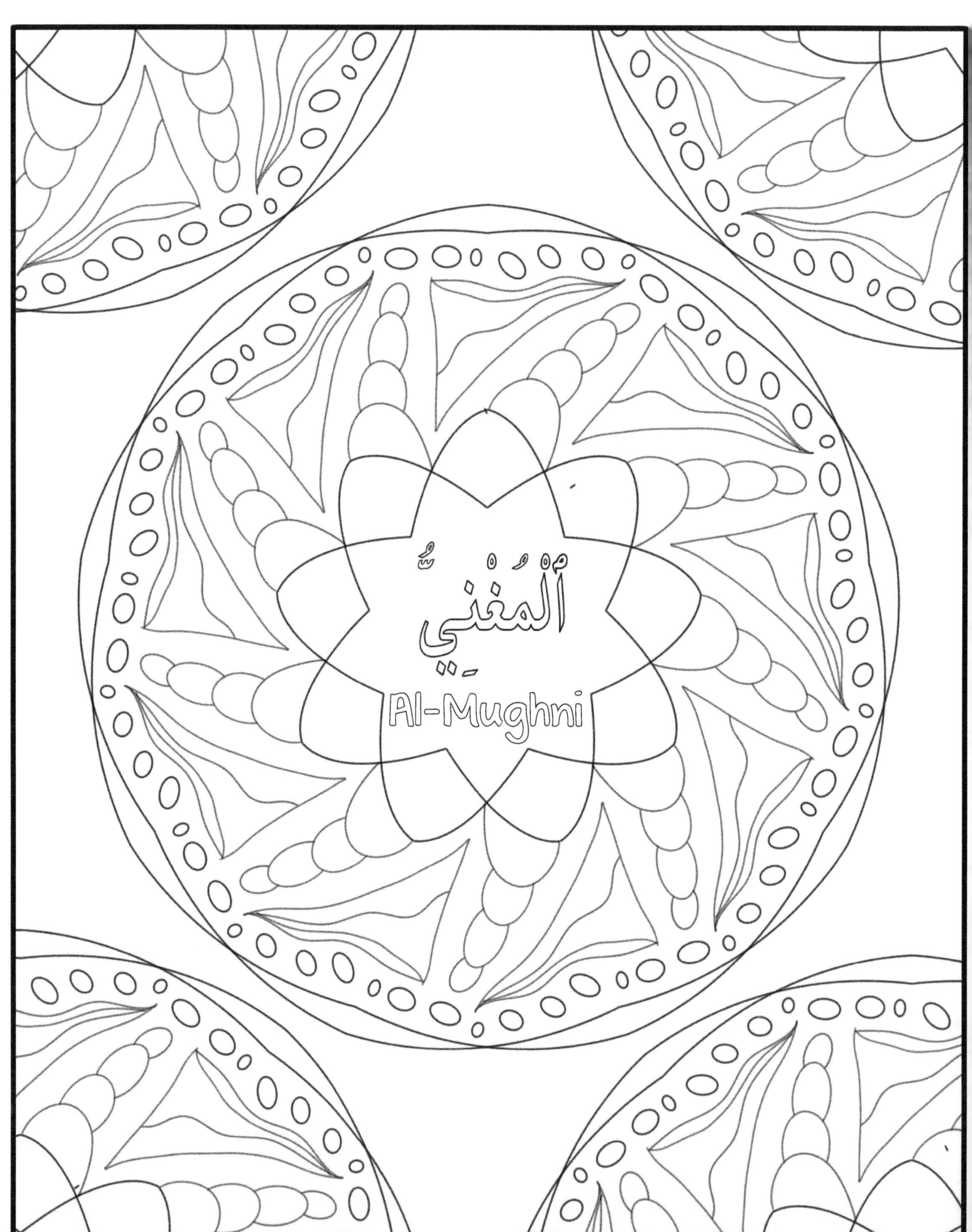

The Preventer

The Withholder.

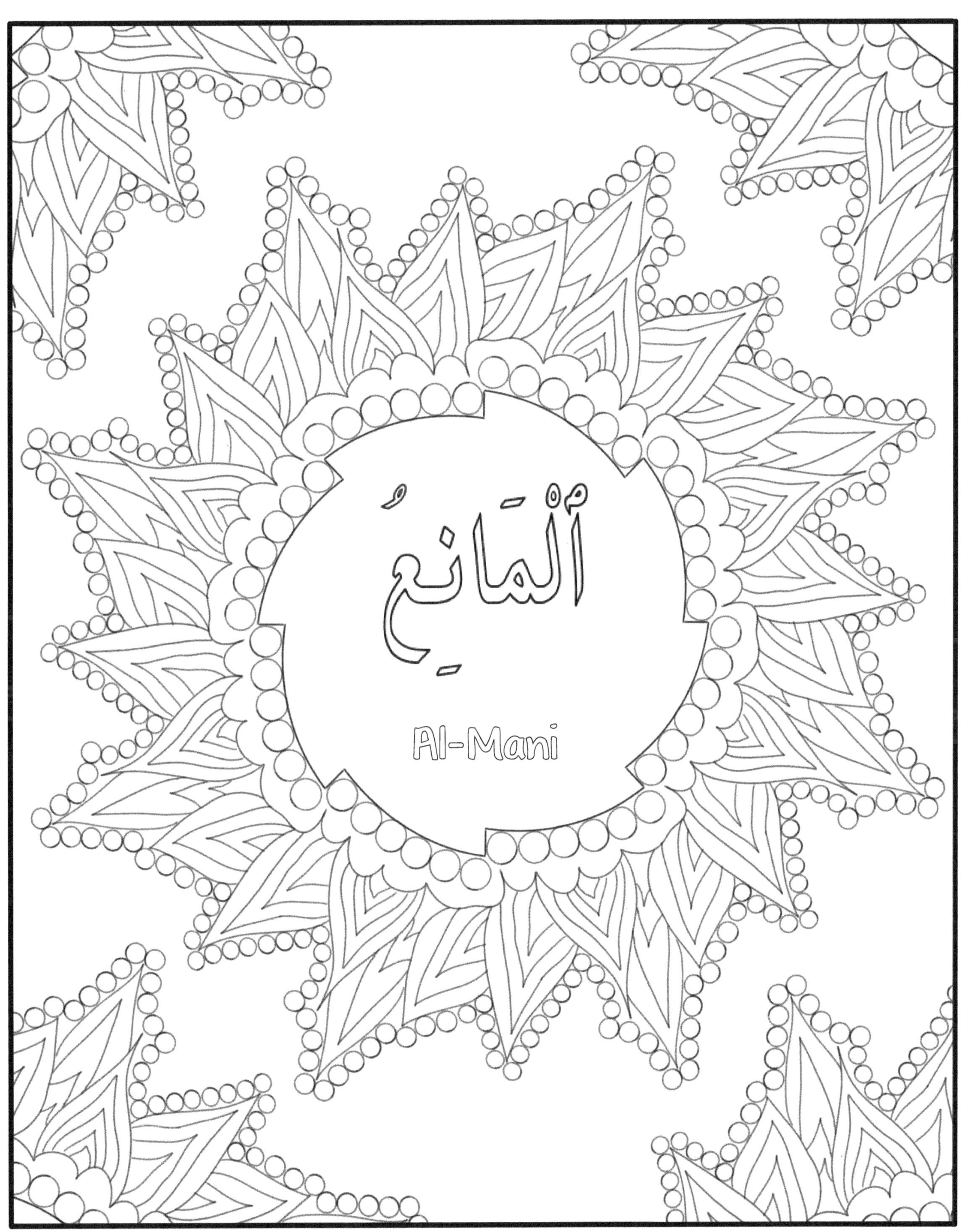

The Distressor

The Correcter, The Balancer, The Afflicter, The Punisher.

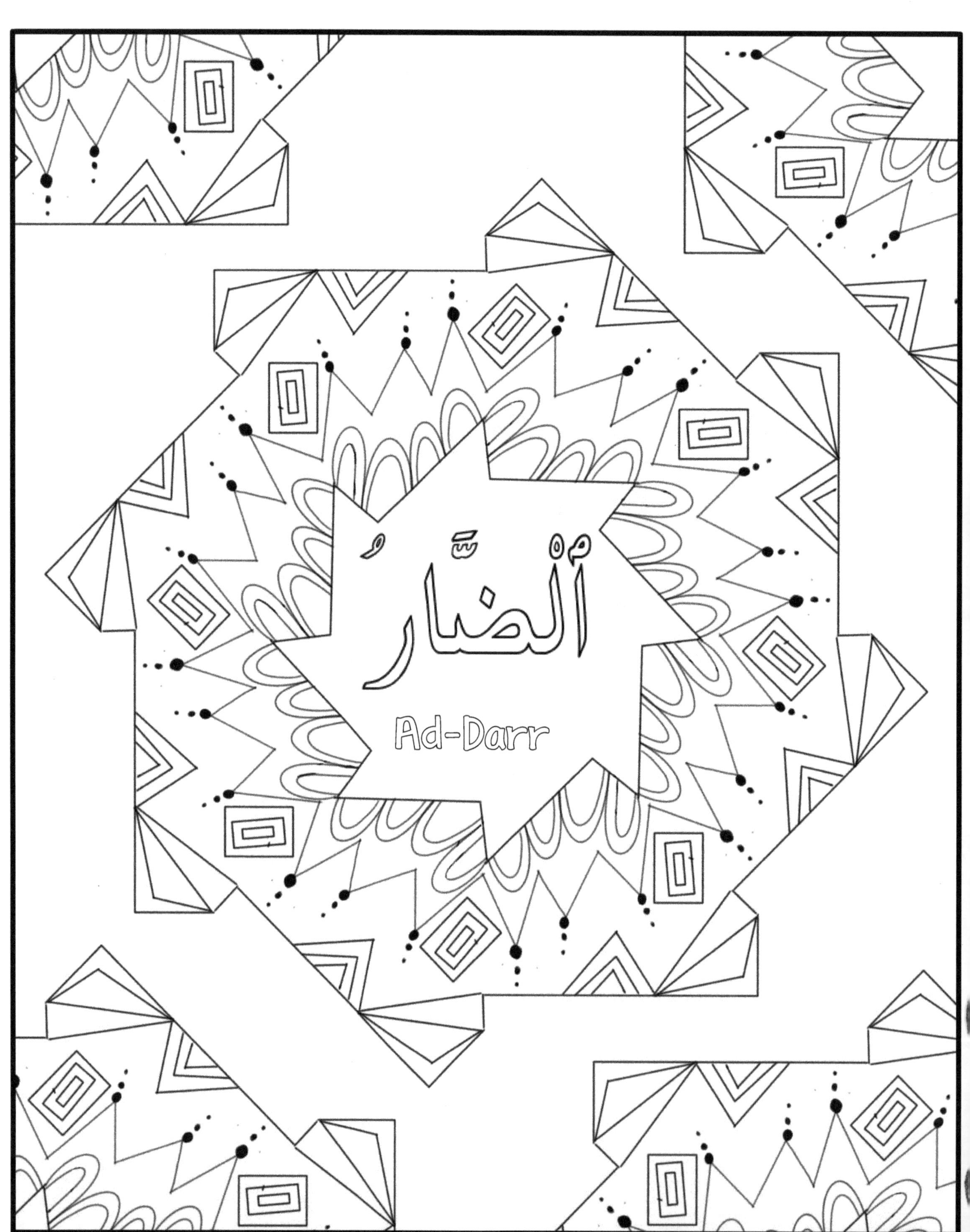

The Bestower of Benefits

The Creator of Good, The Benefiter, The Propitious, The Auspicious

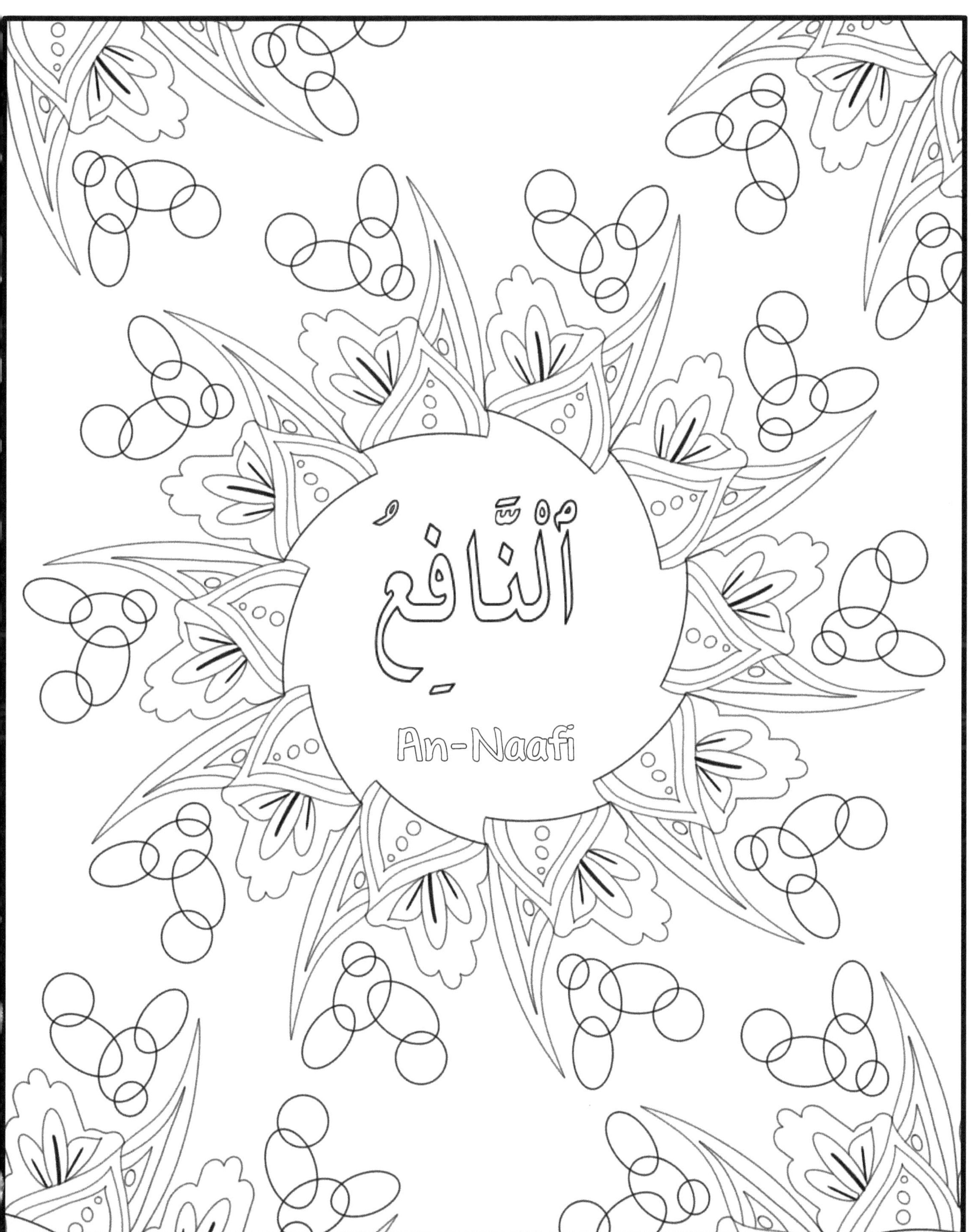

The Prime Light

The Light, The One who guides.

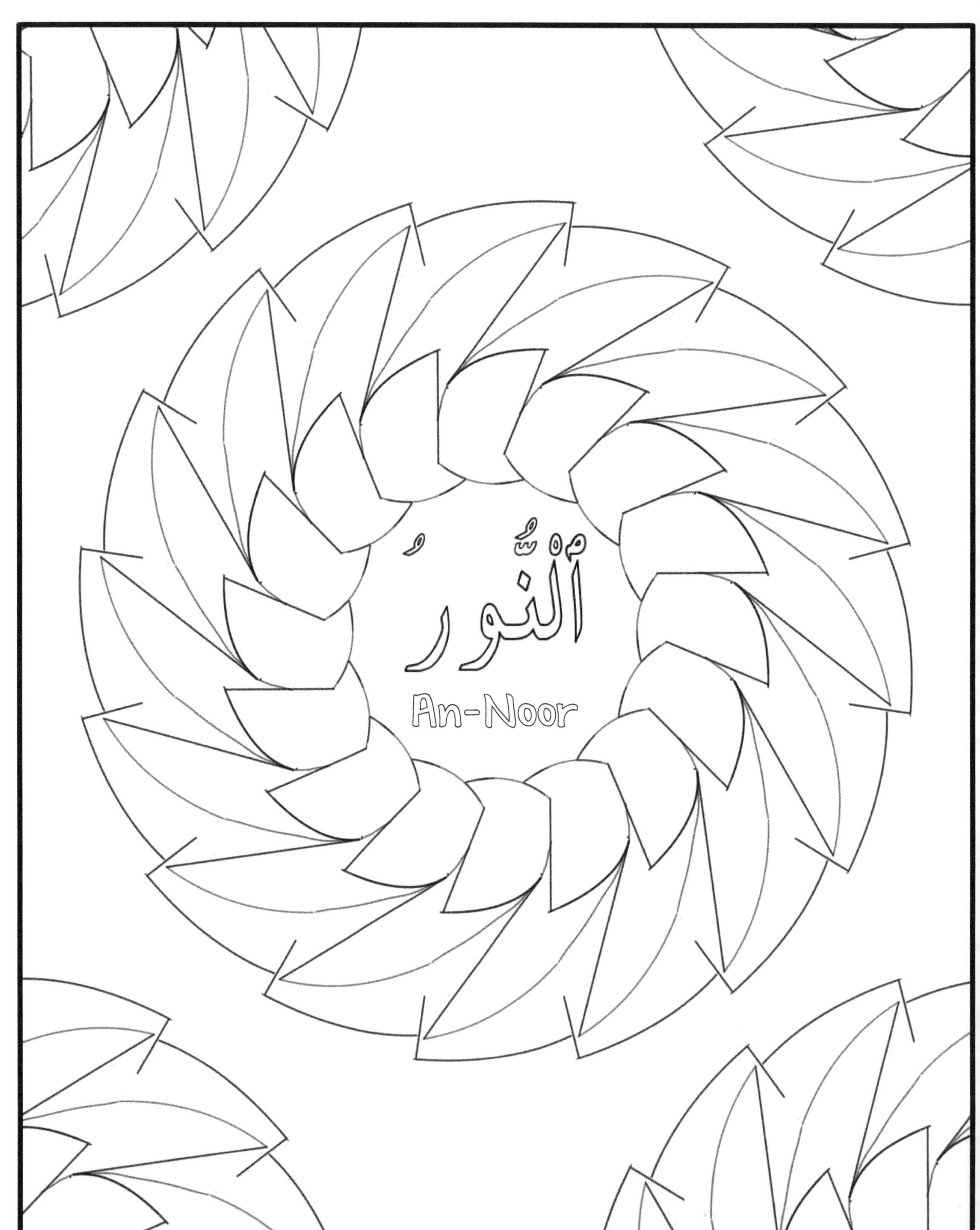

The Provider of Guidance

The Guide, The Leader, The Guide of the Right Path

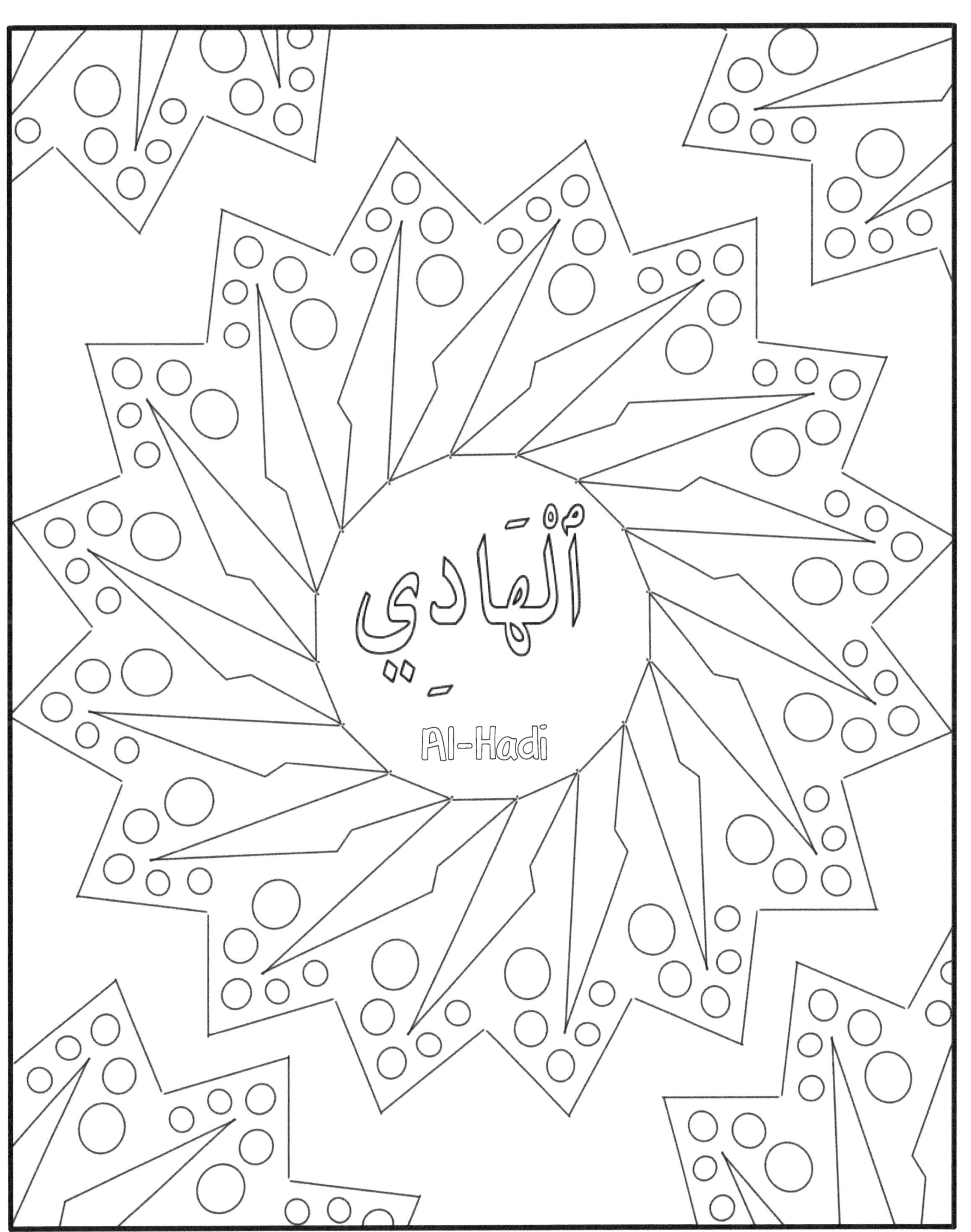

The Unique One

The Wonderful Originator, The Unprecedented and Incomparable

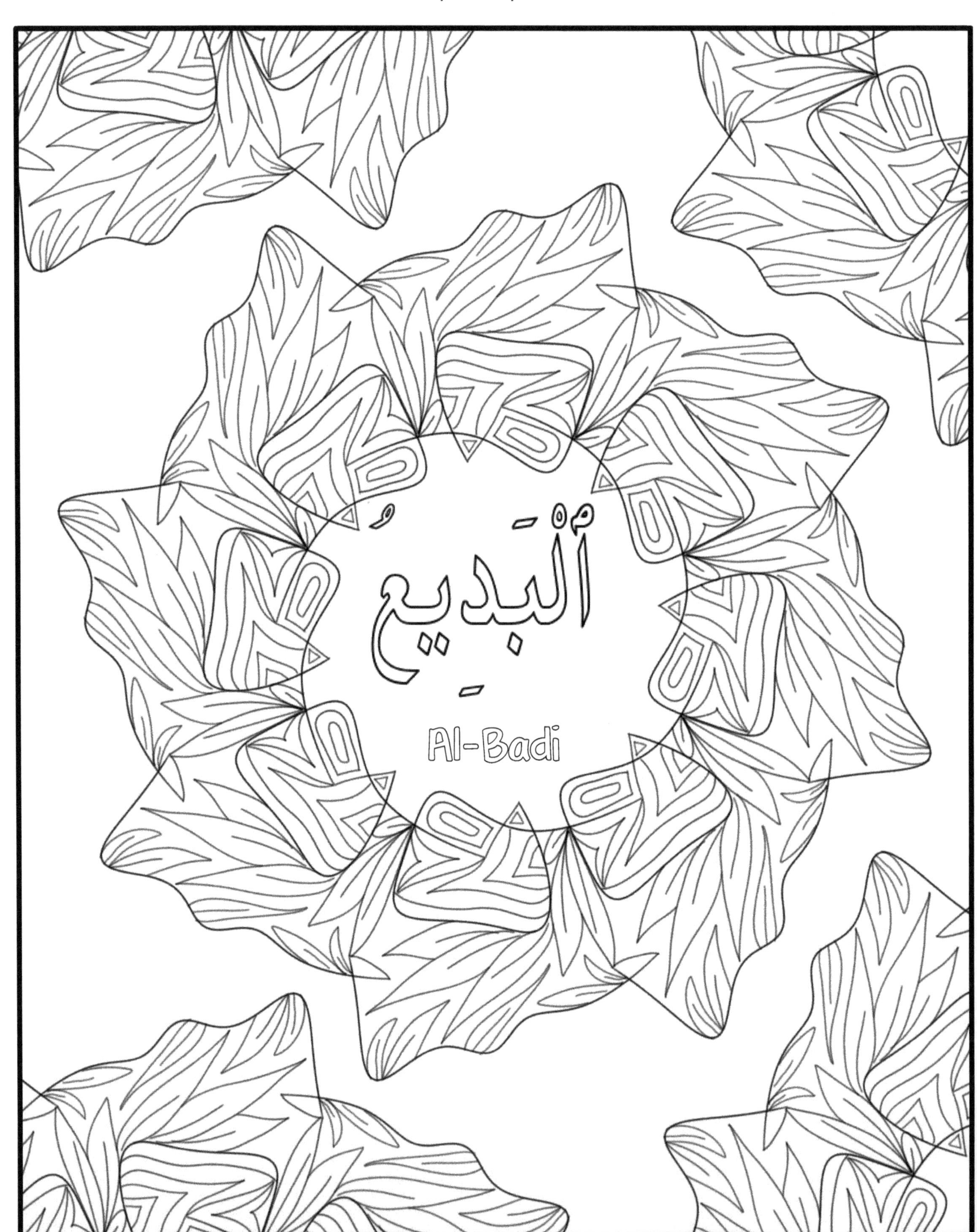

The Ever Surviving One

The Everlasting, The Ever-Enduring, The Ever-Present

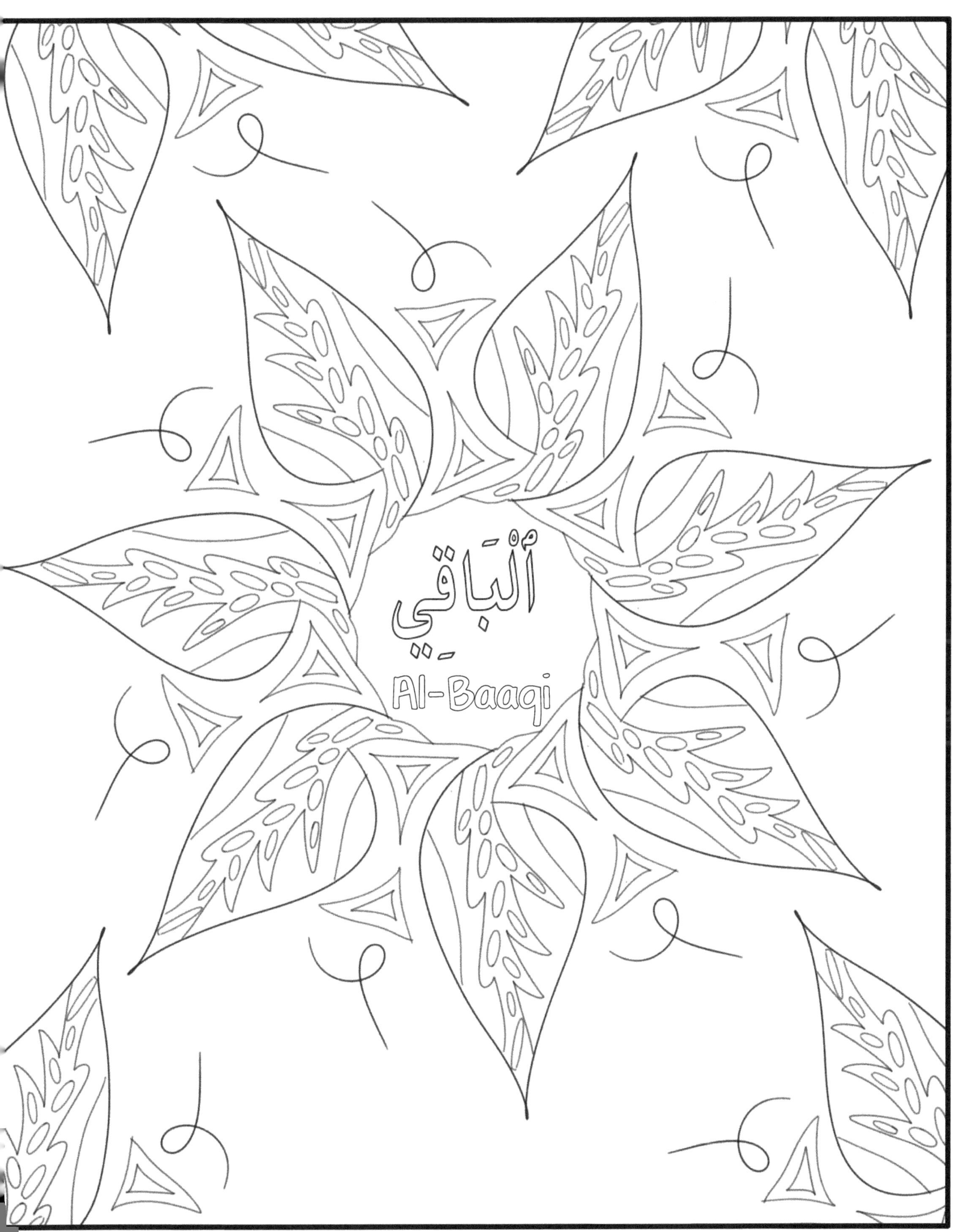

The Internal Inheritor

The Heir, The One whose Existence remains.

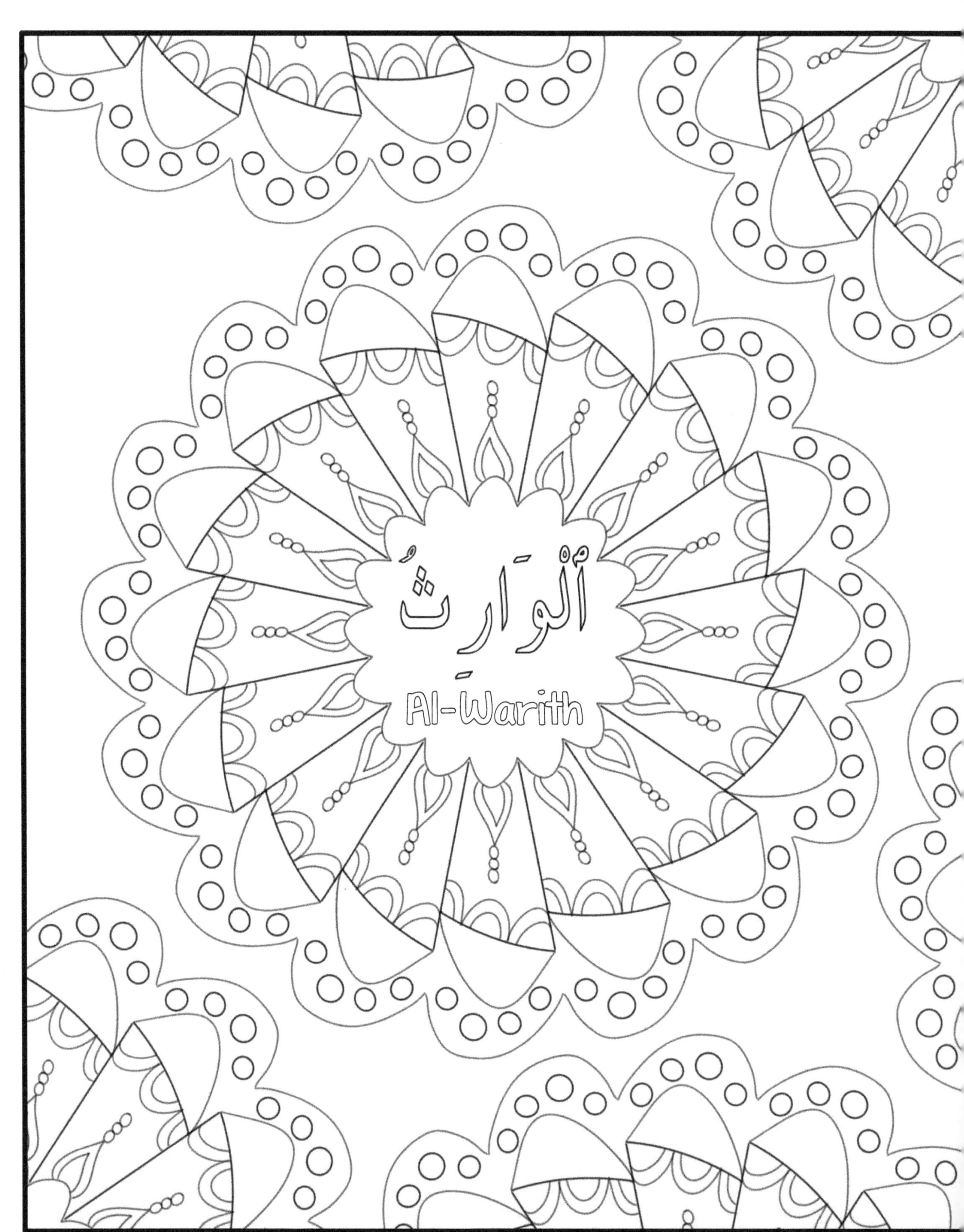

The Guide to the Path of Rectitude

The Guide to the Right Path, The One who guides.

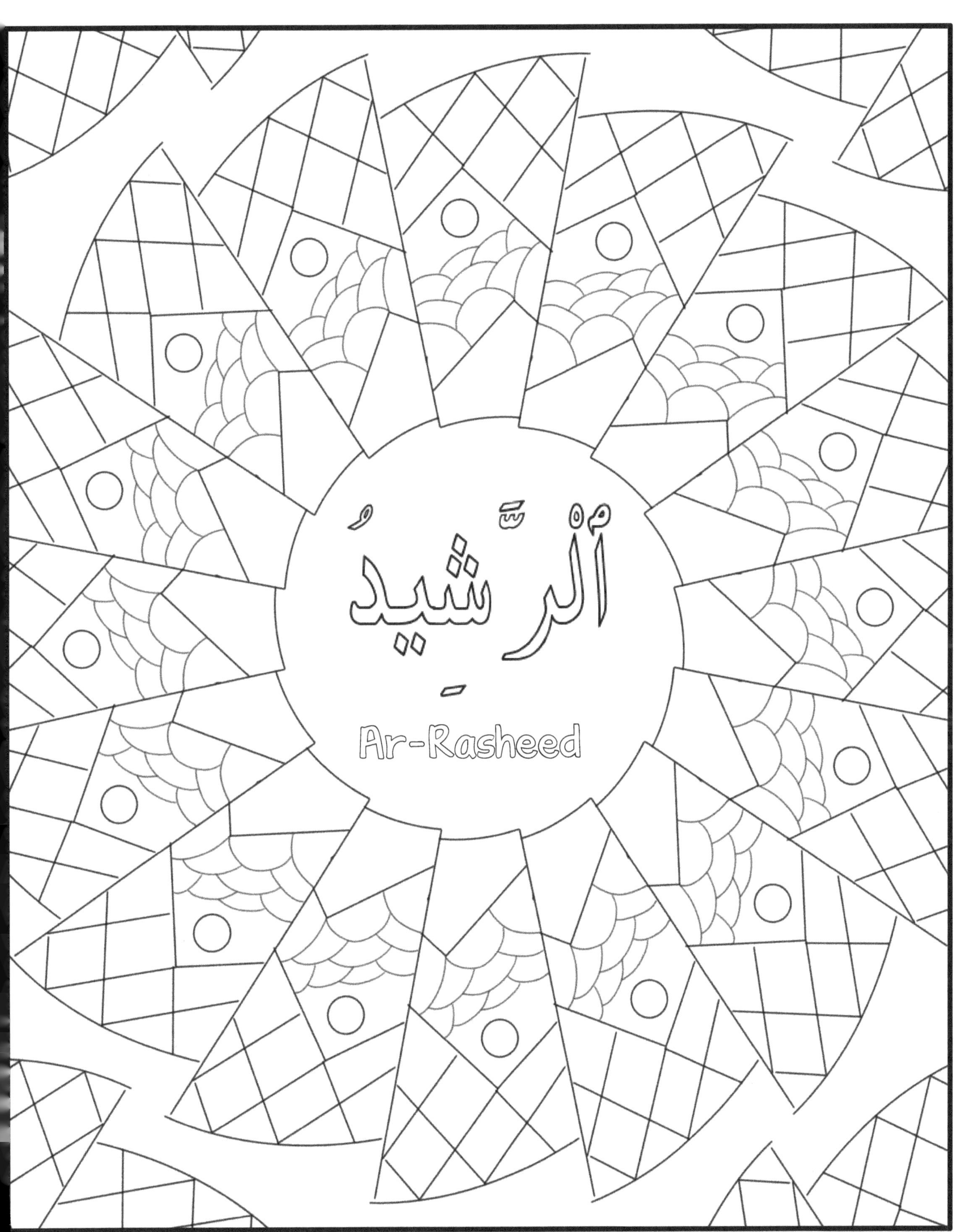

The Extensively Enduring One

The Patient, The One who does not quickly punish the sinners.

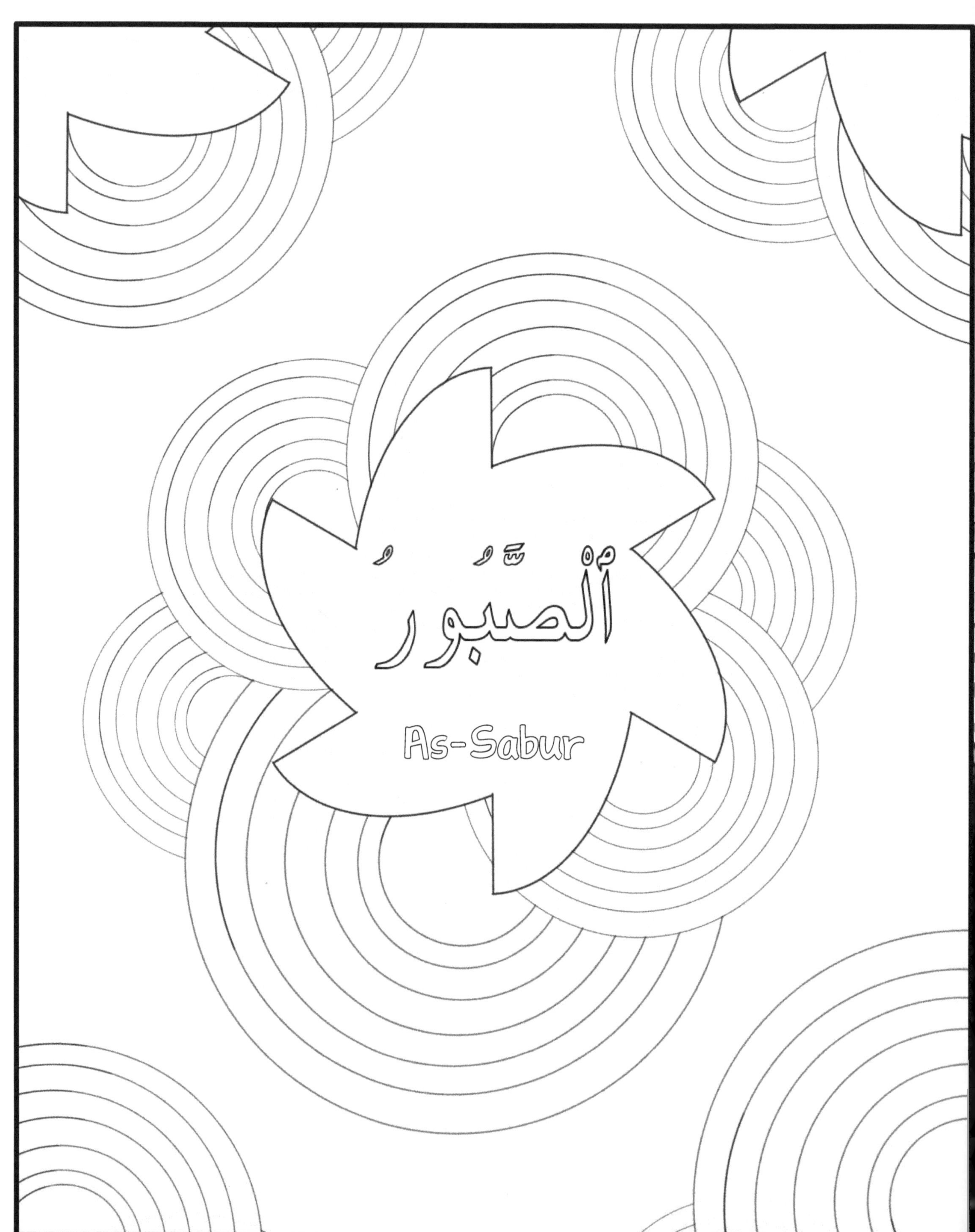

ISBN: 978-0-6455554-5-5

First Published in 2023.

Artwork by Ameera Karimshah

9 780645 555455